The inter-war British economy:

A STATISTICAL ABSTRACT

The inter-war British economy:
A STATISTICAL ABSTRACT

Forrest Capie and Michael Collins

Manchester University Press

First published in 1983
by Manchester University Press
at Oxford Road, Manchester M13 9PL, UK
and at 51 Washington Street, Dover, N.H. 03820, USA

British Library cataloguing in publication data

The Inter-war economy.
1. Great Britain – Economic conditions – 1918–1945
I. Capie, Forrest II. Collins, Michael
330.941'082 HC256.3

ISBN 0–7190–0901–4

Library of Congress cataloging in publication data
applied for

number 82–62248

Photoset by Northern Phototypesetting Company, Bolton
Printed in Great Britain at the Alden Press, Oxford

Preface

This collection of statistics developed out of an undergraduate course we both taught, and one continues to teach, at the University of Leeds, on the British economy between the World Wars. Specifically it grew out of an interest in fluctuations in aggregate economic activity and in individual macro-economic variables (especially monetary and trade variables) and the relationship of the latter to turning points in the total. Such an interest forced attention on monthly and quarterly data series which too often were not readily available and were seldom in consistent form over the whole period. The collection of the data was made possible in part by a grant from the Manpower Services Commission that enabled us to employ research assistants: Rahul Desai, Ann Raymond and Andrew Morgan. Karen Bevins provided computing assistance. The British Academy granted us Overseas Visiting Fellowships in 1978 to visit the National Bureau of economic Research in New York and one part of that visit allowed us to supplement and complement our data with material at that time held by the Bureau. We should like to thank both the British Academy and the National Bureau. We are particularly grateful to Geoffrey Moore at the Bureau for his kind assistance. Finally, we thank David Harkness for always being there to solve our computing problems.

F.H.C.
M.C.

We should like to thank Oxford University Press for permission to use material from *Oxford Economic Papers*, The Midland Bank for data in the *Midland Bank Review*, *The Bankers Magazine* for series that appeared in the *Bankers', Insurance Managers' and Agents' Magazine* and *The Economist* for series found there.

Contents

Introduction

All social scientists, but particularly economists and economic historians, increasingly use statistical analysis in their work, in an effort to provide a more rigorous picture and a better understanding of society and the workings of the economy. This trend is in part a general move towards quantification in social science, a consequence of the availability of improved statistical methods and the rapid speed of calculation made possible by electronic computers. For social scientists the manipulation of large amounts of data within a realistic time period is now not uncommon. In the field of economics this has generated a demand from researchers for more data. For econometricians, and historians using their techniques, much research requires as a starting point the ready availability of consistent data series; and for the study of economic relationships it is often essential that data series should extend over a fairly long time period and have as great a frequency as possible. The function of this book is to make available a wide range of consistent economic time series relating to Britain, over the years 1919 to 1939.

A number of excellent collections of economic time series already exist, but they either provide only annual data or are very selective in their coverage. Thus, the four major publications of historical data covering broad sectors of the economy are: B. R. Mitchell and P. Deane, *Abstract of British Historical Statistics* (Cambridge University Press, 1962); B. R. Mitchell and H. G. Jones, *Second Abstract of British Historical Statistics* (Cambridge University Press, 1971); C. H. Feinstein, *National Income, Expenditure and Output of the United Kingdom 1855–1965* (Cambridge University Press, 1972); and *The British Economy: Key Statistics 1900–1970* (London and Cambridge Economic Service, London 1971); and all these provide annual data only. Even collections that deal solely with one or two economic sectors such as *British Labour Statistics: Historical Abstract 1886–1968* (Department of Employment and Productivity, HMSO, London 1971) and D. K. Sheppard, *The Growth and Role of U.K. Financial Institutions 1880–1962*

(Methuen and Co. Ltd 1971) almost always confine themselves to annual series. For many types of time series analysis, however, data with a greater frequency than each year are preferable. This is obviously true for studies of the nature of seasonal influences on economic variables; and is generally the case for the detailed examination of business or trade cycle fluctuations. Sub-annual data are also a significant improvement over annual data for any research that seeks to establish the timing relationship between movements in different variables; or where calculations allow for timing leads and lags of less than one year. Also in econometric investigations larger numbers of observations allow greater degrees of freedom and facilitate estimation of parameters. In other words the use of sub-annual data is basic to a very broad range of economic and historical research. For this reason the data series in this book are all sub-annual – monthly and quarterly series. As such, they are intended partly to supplement existing collections of British economic data for the inter-war years, but at the same time to be a useful independent collection of statistics.

The series have been drawn from diverse sources, some more accessible than others but none easily available to the researcher. The most important published source has been the *Ministry of Labour Gazette* which was established in 1893 and appeared as a monthly throughout the period. The *Gazette* published many series relating to wages, employment, unemployment and prices, with details on coverage and reliability of the series and with special articles offering analysis of the figures and providing descriptions of methods of compilation. Similarly, we have drawn on the *Board of Trade Journal* for its series on industrial production and for informed comment on the *Trade and Navigation Accounts*. Although still formally a private institution, the Bank of England from 1932 provided through its *Statistical Summary* a collection of general economic data, relating especially to capital and money markets, and this too has been made use of. *The Economist* has been another major source both for individual series and for articles that discuss the coverage and reliability of official series. However, the contemporary publication that deserves special mention for its careful appraisals of these series is the (monthly) *London and Cambridge Economic Service Bulletin* (from 1927 the data tables also appeared in the *Royal Economic Society's Memoranda*). The *Journal of the Royal Statistical Society* also occasionally carried discussions of important economic time series, and regularly published a number of official series.

No collection of historical statistics will be ideal. Those presented here relate to broad areas of the economy, but even so, largely because of the restriction to sub-annual data, coverage cannot be completely uniform in terms of time and of the economic sectors represented. Thus, not all the series covered the whole period; and while there are large numbers of monthly time series relating, for instance, to the monetary sector, the Stock Exchange and the labour market, there are exceedingly few series touching on the government sector, capital formation or output of the non-industrial sector.

One other general difficulty arising from the use of economic time series is the existence of 'breaks' in the data as a result of reclassification or extension or changes in base years. The details of such breaks are given in the introduction to individual chapters. Generally, however, if the break was such as to change the whole character of the series – as in the case of fundamental reclassification or shift in definitions or method – then the data are presented in their original form with a description of such changes. In such cases it is up to the researcher to determine how the series can be best adapted to his or her particular purpose. Where different base years were used it has usually been possible to convert to one of them by means of a simple arithmetic transformation based on the overlapping information.

Unless otherwise noted all data relate to the United Kingdom of Great Britain and Northern Ireland, except that Southern Ireland is included until 1922.

In view of the considerable changes in prices after World War I some value series require conversion to constant prices, and where possible all constant price and volume series have been converted to the base year, 1924, even though this was often not the base year used originally. The conversion to 1924 is purely an arithmetic adjustment made possible by overlapping in the original source of data series relating to different base periods.

Finally, in many monthly or quarterly series the problem of

seasonality arises. All series were therefore tested for the presence of seasonal factors (even though *a priori* we would not expect many of them to exhibit such a pattern) and where seasonality was detected the series was adjusted. The procedure was as follows. Two-way analysis of variance was used and F-ratios calculated in the customary way, an arbitrary decision being taken to decide the magnitude of an F-ratio that indicated the presence of seasonality. This was supplemented by visual examination of the graphs of all the individual series. The method selected for the calculation of seasonal indices used in deseasonalising the raw series depends upon how it is believed seasonal variations interact with other variations in the time series. If the seasonal variations are believed to be constant over the cycle, an additive model would be appropriate; whereas if they were a constant proportion of trend and cyclical movements a multiplicative model would be more appropriate. In view of the strong cyclical nature of the data in this period the multiplicative model was adopted. This was vindicated by testing a sample of the series by means of the recently developed techniques of the Central Statistical Office[1] and it was this method that was used for carrying out the seasonal adjustment. A final test was carried out on a sample of the deseasonalised data. The two-way analysis of variance was again used and the wholly insignificant F-ratios obtained confirmed the removal of the seasonal element.

NOTE

1 A description of the technique can be found in J. Durbin and M. J. Murphy, 'Seasonal adjustment based on a mixed additive–multiplicative model', *Journal of the Royal Statistical Society*, series A CXXXVIII (1975) Ch. 3, pp. 385–410. We would like to thank the Central Statistical Office for making their computer program available and for helpful guidance.

1 Production

TABLES

SOURCES

Tables 1.1–1.16 *London and Cambridge Economic Service Bulletin*
Tables 1.17–1.36 *Board of Trade Journal*

One of the most important and potentially useful collections of series for the economist and historian for any period is that of disaggregated production. Where available in sub-annual form, production figures provide a good guide to the trend in total output; and in disaggregated form, the course of activity for industrial sub-groupings. In aggregate they are not a perfect substitute for the *course* of total output but are nevertheless a good proxy since many major services tend to mirror the movements in industrial output.

There are two sets of sub-annual production data on a quarterly basis for the inter-war years. One is that provided by the London and Cambridge Economic Service covering almost the whole period

(1920–38), and the other that produced by the Board of Trade for the shorter period 1928 to mid-1939. As can be seen from the table headings the sub-groups of these two collections are not strictly comparable. The Board of Trade series are more extensive in their coverage (both within each group and in the number of groups provided) so that the totals of the indices are not strictly comparable either, though the paths of both do in fact move quite closely together. It is surprising how little used these series have been and indeed how little known they have been, for their coverage, while not complete, is useful for many purposes and as reliable as many other more frequently used series.

The London and Cambridge series provides figures in index form with the base being average quarterly production in 1924. The sub-groups were based on the groups in the 1907 Census of Production and the weights used were based on the relative importance of each group in the total. The weights were revised with the fresh information contained in each census of production.

There are certain advantages, but also some disadvantages, in using the quarterly index. The principal advantage is obviously the greater frequency. There are others too, for instance, in the sub-group shipbuilding, the annual index used *tonnage launched* whereas the quarterly index used *tonnage under construction*. The latter clearly affords a better indication of the level of activity. The chief disadvantage is that the quarterly index has a lesser coverage than the annual because of the unavailability of data. The following table shows the differences between the two series.

ANNUAL	QUARTERLY
Group I **Mines and quarries** – production of principal minerals.	**Minerals** – production of coal only is available.
Group II **Iron and steel, engineering and shipbuilding trades** – production of iron and steel tin plate, galvanised sheets, exports	**Iron and steel, engineering and shipbuilding** – production of pig-iron and steel. For shipbuilding, tonnage under

ANNUAL – contd.

Group II – contd.
of railway locomotives and railway wheels and axles, tonnage of ships launched.

Group III
Metal trades other than iron and steel – copper, lead, tin and zinc; home smelter output and total metal manufactured.

Group IV
Textile trades – separate series for cotton, wool, jute, hemp and linen, silk and lace manufacture, based mainly on the trade returns of imports and exports at various stages.

QUARTERLY – contd.

construction has been taken, and not tonnage launched as for the annual index.

Non-ferrous metal trades – home smelter outputs are not obtainable quarterly, nor is the production of home ores. The only available indicator for the home smelting industry is, therefore, the net imports of ores. In the case of copper, for which alone the smelter output from imported ores is really important, the ore imports have been added to the net imports of metal less UK exports, corrected for changes in port stocks in accordance with the London metal exchange returns since 1920. One series is calculated for copper and one for lead, tin and zinc as in the annual index.

Textile manufacture – for the cotton trade a series based on raw material consumed has been used, as the method adopted in the annual index is not applicable to so short a period as a quarter.

The absence of any information whatsoever in regard to stocks of wool, jute,

ANNUAL – contd.

Group IV – contd.

QUARTERLY – contd.

hemp and linen makes a quarterly index impracticable.

In the silk trade the position is altogether different, and though changes in stocks are not known, the method employed for the annual index may reasonably be used.

Without further experience the method used for the annual index of the lace trade is not considered sufficiently reliable for quarterly use.

Group V

Food, drink and tobacco trades – separate series for grain milling, total flour consumption, sugar refining, cocoa and tobacco manufacture – all based on the trade returns – and the production of beer and spirits.

Food, drink and tobacco manufacture – all the series used in the annual index are available quarterly with the exception of spirits and beer. Since 1920 the production of beer has been considerably less than in pre-war years; sugar is excluded by way of effecting some sort of balance. The series taken for this group, therefore, are flour, cocoa and tobacco consumption.

Group VI

Chemical and allied trades – production of soda-ash (supplied by Messrs Brunner, Mond & Co. Ltd.), sulphuric acid and coal tar. Net imports of oil seeds and phosphate of lime.

Chemical manufacture – Mond supplied a quarterly as well as an annual index of their production of soda-ash. No quarterly statistics are available for the production of coal tar and

ANNUAL – contd.	QUARTERLY – contd.
	pitch, or of sulphuric acid, but the net imports of iron pyrites give some indications as to the latter, and have been utilised. The series for seed-crushing and fertilisers can be calculated from the trade returns.
Group VII **Paper, printing and allied trades** – net imports of raw materials reduced to their paper-making equivalents.	**Paper, printing, etc.** – the series can be calculated from the trade returns in the same way as for the annual index.
Group VIII **Leather trades** – net imports of raw materials reduced to their leather content.	**Leather** – no quarterly index is obtainable.
Group IX **Indiarubber trades** – net imports of crude rubber, gutta-percha and Balata.	**Rubber** – quarterly imports were unsatisfactory.
Group X **Timber trades** – net imports of timber.	**Timber** – quarterly imports were unsatisfactory.
Group XI **Clay, stone, building and contracting trades** – represented in part by production of cement.	**Production of cement** – not available quarterly.

The annual LCES index omitted altogether the rapidly growing gas, water and electricity supply and building materials and timber products. It also omitted clothing (which was not a rapidly growing group) although for the textile group the weighting was adjusted to make allowance for the clothing trades; and it overestimated the increase in metal products.[1] All of this was allowed for in the more comprehensive annual index compiled by Lomax.[2]

Clearly there are fewer series available in quarterly form and further, several are estimates made on the basis of imports of the appropriate raw material. The latter introduces a slight bias suggesting output levels for dates earlier than actually realised.[3] The major omissions from the annual index are agriculture, leather, rubber, timber and cement. All the series are given in raw and seasonally adjusted form.

The Board of Trade series were compiled in a similar fashion to that of LCES but had the advantage of being able to include additional data from official or other confidential sources. The figures for 1928–33 were originally presented as a percentage of the average for 1924 and those for 1934–9 were expressed as a percentage of the 1930 average. In the series given here all figures have been converted to a 1924 base. The weights used were based on 'value added' in the most recent census of production. Information on industries was drawn from official returns of trade, and wages and production from a wide range of sources. The initial index was thought to cover two-thirds of productive activity of manufacturing and mining in Great Britain and Northern Ireland. The index was revised in 1935 when one important deficiency of the old index was remedied, namely the inclusion of the construction of new buildings. The remaining important omissions were clothing other than boots and shoes, and public utility services other than gas and electricity. The revised index covered more than seventy per cent of activity in the manufacturing and mining sectors and over ninety per cent of activity in the trades listed.[4] The total included various industries not provided separately: production of pianos, paper and the consumption of rubber.

NOTES

1 See Feinstein *op. cit.* for further discussion.

2 K. S. Lomax, 'Production and productivity movements in the United Kingdom since 1900', *JRSS*, CXXII, (1959).

3 Full details can be found in the *London and Cambridge Economic Service Bulletin*, VII, 4, 23 April 1929.

4 A full description of the old index is given in *Board of Trade Journal*, 28 March 1935.

TABLE 1.1 : QUARTERLY INDEX OF PRODUCTION (LONDON & CAMBRIDGE) : GROUP1
(1924 AVERAGE = 100)

	MAR	JUN	SEP	DEC
1920	92.3	86.4	88.0	72.4
1921	80.6	0.3	77.9	85.3
1922	92.4	85.5	94.1	102.1
1923	105.5	103.6	98.2	106.4
1924	107.3	99.3	95.0	98.4
1925	100.8	87.8	83.6	94.4
1926	102.5	29.8	10.4	41.6
1927	100.0	93.5	90.8	94.1
1928	97.1	86.1	83.8	91.4
1929	101.2	93.1	93.3	99.5
1930	104.2	87.8	83.7	91.6
1931	88.3	81.4	76.2	86.2
1932	85.4	78.8	69.3	83.9
1933	85.5	73.0	71.1	84.4
1934	90.5	79.6	77.6	86.4
1935	89.4	80.5	78.0	89.3
1936	93.0	81.7	81.5	89.1
1937	93.8	92.3	86.5	93.7
1938	97.6	82.2	79.0	89.3

TABLE 1.2 : QUARTERLY INDEX OF PRODUCTION (LONDON & CAMBRIDGE) : GROUP1
SEAONALLY ADJUSTED (1924 AVERAGE = 100)

	MAR	JUN	SEP	DEC
1920	75	113	92	65
1921	66	0	81	76
1922	76	112	98	91
1923	86	136	103	95
1924	88	130	99	88
1925	82	115	87	84
1926	84	39	11	37
1927	82	122	95	84
1928	79	113	87	82
1929	83	122	97	89
1930	85	115	87	82
1931	72	107	80	77
1932	70	103	72	75
1933	70	96	74	76
1934	74	104	81	77
1935	73	105	81	80
1936	76	107	85	80
1937	77	121	90	84
1938	80	108	82	80

TABLE 1.3 : QUARTERLY INDEX OF PRODUCTION (LONDON & CAMBRIDGE) : GROUP2
(1924 AVERAGE = 100)

	MAR	JUN	SEP	DEC
1920	157.4	167.8	161.2	150.2
1921	139.0	85.2	97.0	88.0
1922	86.7	78.6	80.5	87.2
1923	103.6	110.6	91.5	104.4
1924	109.0	106.2	94.6	90.6
1925	95.1	89.2	79.4	81.1
1926	92.8	49.4	25.1	32.7
1927	103.4	116.0	111.3	112.0
1928	110.1	107.7	94.9	100.8
1929	109.1	114.8	116.4	115.9
1930	118.1	104.1	85.2	72.9
1931	63.2	55.8	49.1	50.1
1932	50.9	46.2	42.3	44.9
1933	50.7	58.6	59.7	66.2
1934	75.6	81.5	78.2	82.0
1935	84.0	93.4	94.7	98.2
1936	106.5	108.8	108.7	114.0
1937	115.7	122.4	125.1	130.5
1938	125.0	107.3	86.4	91.0

TABLE 1.4 : QUARTERLY INDEX OF PRODUCTION (LONDON & CAMBRIDGE) : GROUP2
SEASONALLY ADJUSTED(1924 AVERAGE = 100)

	MAR	JUN	SEP	DEC
1920	146	165	172	155
1921	129	84	103	91
1922	80	77	86	90
1923	96	109	98	107
1924	101	104	101	93
1925	88	88	85	83
1926	86	49	27	34
1927	96	114	119	115
1928	102	106	101	104
1929	101	113	124	119
1930	110	102	91	75
1931	59	55	52	52
1932	47	45	45	46
1933	47	58	64	68
1934	70	80	83	84
1935	78	92	101	101
1936	99	107	116	117
1937	107	120	133	134
1938	116	105	92	94

TABLE 1.5 : QUARTERLY INDEX OF PRODUCTION (LONDON & CAMBRIDGE) : GROUP3
(1924 AVERAGE = 100)

	MAR	JUN	SEP	DEC
1920	86.9	65.2	93.0	77.3
1921	60.4	64.7	58.4	55.8
1922	55.9	55.2	69.9	65.4
1923	87.0	86.3	87.0	96.6
1924	96.6	90.4	111.6	101.2
1925	100.0	102.6	111.2	110.3
1926	117.6	103.8	114.4	119.2
1927	125.9	123.5	118.7	119.8
1928	117.5	122.9	106.9	112.1
1929	111.5	120.5	117.7	114.7
1930	111.8	117.2	114.3	119.4
1931	92.4	121.9	101.0	110.6
1932	105.9	95.5	92.0	99.3
1933	87.3	115.9	110.1	123.3
1934	139.3	142.3	147.2	166.8
1935	162.7	177.3	145.9	157.2
1936	156.6	165.4	173.3	172.7
1937	175.4	191.3	187.9	178.8
1938	163.4	166.5	160.2	159.5

TABLE 1.6 : QUARTERLY INDEX OF PRODUCTION (LONDON & CAMBRIDGE) : GROUP3
SEASONALLY ADJUSTED(1924 AVERAGE = 100)

	MAR	JUN	SEP	DEC
1920	89	64	93	77
1921	62	64	58	55
1922	57	55	70	65
1923	89	85	87	96
1924	99	89	111	101
1925	102	101	111	110
1926	120	103	114	118
1927	129	122	118	119
1928	120	121	107	111
1929	114	119	117	114
1930	114	116	114	119
1931	94	120	101	110
1932	108	94	92	99
1933	89	115	110	123
1934	142	141	147	166
1935	166	175	145	156
1936	160	163	173	172
1937	179	189	187	178
1938	167	165	160	159

TABLE 1.7 : QUARTERLY INDEX OF PRODUCTION (LONDON & CAMBRIDGE) : GROUP4
(1924 AVERAGE = 100)

	MAR	JUN	SEP	DEC
1920	144.6	88.6	95.1	97.6
1921	58.3	39.5	86.4	101.4
1922	101.5	109.1	111.2	111.9
1923	100.9	79.4	76.2	115.5
1924	101.0	90.8	83.2	125.3
1925	134.2	124.0	99.5	129.0
1926	130.4	102.1	82.2	107.0
1927	139.0	118.2	108.2	113.5
1928	118.4	112.0	98.1	119.7
1929	120.8	114.7	94.1	124.5
1930	112.9	90.6	68.4	87.7
1931	79.3	84.8	82.1	110.2
1932	111.6	107.2	85.2	100.5
1933	108.2	102.7	107.3	119.5
1934	121.1	111.9	101.1	115.4
1935	120.7	119.9	111.2	127.1
1936	132.0	128.7	122.6	128.6
1937	139.6	146.1	134.0	137.3
1938	132.7	104.3	100.5	109.5

TABLE 1.8 : QUARTERLY INDEX OF PRODUCTION (LONDON & CAMBRIDGE) : GROUP4
SEASONALLY ADJUSTED(1924 AVERAGE = 100)

	MAR	JUN	SEP	DEC
1920	136	92	105	90
1921	55	41	95	94
1922	96	114	123	103
1923	95	83	84	107
1924	96	96	92	116
1925	126	129	110	119
1926	123	106	91	99
1927	131	123	119	105
1928	111	117	108	111
1929	114	120	104	115
1930	106	94	75	81
1931	75	88	91	102
1932	105	112	94	93
1933	102	107	118	110
1934	114	117	112	107
1935	114	125	123	117
1936	124	134	135	119
1937	131	152	148	127
1938	125	109	111	101

TABLE 1.9 : QUARTERLY INDEX OF PRODUCTION (LONDON & CAMBRIDGE) : GROUP5
(1924 AVERAGE = 100)

	MAR	JUN	SEP	DEC
1920	98.6	92.8	102.2	86.6
1921	81.6	98.2	100.3	90.3
1922	89.2	96.4	107.2	85.2
1923	91.1	95.0	94.0	95.0
1924	92.5	97.8	104.9	104.8
1925	94.8	97.8	96.0	99.4
1926	95.3	98.6	97.8	96.8
1927	105.7	101.4	104.2	101.6
1928	104.4	99.3	103.5	104.2
1929	101.9	110.6	111.3	107.9
1930	99.8	110.3	109.3	117.1
1931	115.3	103.8	118.1	115.2
1932	117.2	111.7	107.0	111.9
1933	112.8	112.3	104.2	112.5
1934	116.3	117.4	112.2	114.8
1935	108.3	123.1	115.1	123.9
1936	119.7	132.4	120.9	130.3
1937	121.4	131.7	119.3	125.0
1938	118.0	128.4	127.0	131.4

TABLE 1.10 : QUARTERLY INDEX OF PRODUCTION (LONDON & CAMBRIDGE) : GROUP5
SEASONALLY ADJUSTED(1924 AVERAGE = 100)

	MAR	JUN	SEP	DEC
1920	101	91	101	87
1921	84	97	99	90
1922	91	95	106	85
1923	93	94	93	95
1924	95	96	104	105
1925	97	96	95	99
1926	98	97	97	97
1927	108	100	103	102
1928	107	98	102	104
1929	104	109	110	108
1930	102	109	108	117
1931	118	102	117	115
1932	120	110	106	112
1933	115	111	103	113
1934	119	116	111	115
1935	111	121	114	124
1936	123	130	120	130
1937	124	130	118	125
1938	121	127	126	132

TABLE 1.11 : QUARTERLY INDEX OF PRODUCTION (LONDON & CAMBRIDGE) : GROUP6
(1924 AVERAGE = 100)

	MAR	JUN	SEP	DEC
1920	97.8	119.0	105.0	114.7
1921	87.3	33.8	61.6	90.6
1922	83.9	93.7	87.8	96.4
1923	105.7	90.3	81.2	87.2
1924	95.4	103.0	101.0	101.2
1925	107.6	94.4	82.4	87.4
1926	90.0	79.5	72.6	84.4
1927	107.0	92.6	92.8	97.9
1928	104.8	103.8	93.3	102.7
1929	100.1	102.1	103.4	105.4
1930	94.5	88.8	97.7	84.2
1931	83.9	82.5	73.9	86.5
1932	89.2	96.1	81.8	90.1
1933	88.0	94.1	84.4	101.1
1934	103.7	96.7	91.6	103.8
1935	107.7	102.3	99.6	120.5
1936	112.8	113.3	104.7	116.4
1937	127.7	125.8	116.1	123.4
1938	114.2	103.7	98.5	116.9

TABLE 1.12 : QUARTERLY INDEX OF PRODUCTION (LONDON & CAMBRIDGE) : GROUP6
SEASONALLY ADJUSTED(1924 AVERAGE = 100)

	MAR	JUN	SEP	DEC
1920	93	123	111	110
1921	83	35	65	87
1922	80	97	93	92
1923	101	93	86	84
1924	91	106	107	97
1925	102	98	87	84
1926	86	82	77	81
1927	102	96	98	94
1928	100	107	99	99
1929	95	105	110	101
1930	90	92	104	81
1931	80	85	78	83
1932	85	99	87	86
1933	84	97	89	97
1934	99	100	97	100
1935	103	106	106	116
1936	107	117	111	112
1937	122	130	123	118
1938	109	107	104	112

TABLE 1.13 : QUARTERLY INDEX OF PRODUCTION (LONDON & CAMBRIDGE) : GROUP7
(1924 AVERAGE = 100)

	MAR	JUN	SEP	DEC
1920	71.8	104.8	105.1	83.1
1921	33.5	25.3	66.9	49.4
1922	35.7	70.2	94.8	77.5
1923	71.4	92.5	116.5	88.3
1924	53.7	104.9	127.2	114.2
1925	77.3	99.4	108.6	111.2
1926	91.7	114.4	114.8	103.5
1927	109.0	112.1	126.4	124.2
1928	82.4	118.0	99.8	122.9
1929	111.2	136.6	139.7	147.0
1930	116.3	127.0	125.4	122.5
1931	101.6	94.0	121.1	142.6
1932	143.1	101.5	136.5	155.6
1933	126.6	138.4	144.8	147.2
1934	144.3	170.8	155.4	168.0
1935	144.4	154.2	155.7	187.3
1936	155.0	177.5	173.9	188.6
1937	127.2	152.0	153.3	182.4
1938	161.0	125.0	115.7	150.0

TABLE 1.14 : QUARTERLY INDEX OF PRODUCTION (LONDON & CAMBRIDGE) : GROUP7
SEASONALLY ADJUSTED(1924 AVERAGE = 100)

	MAR	JUN	SEP	DEC
1920	84	108	95	76
1921	39	26	60	45
1922	42	72	86	71
1923	84	95	105	81
1924	64	109	116	106
1925	91	102	98	102
1926	107	118	104	95
1927	128	115	114	114
1928	97	121	90	113
1929	130	140	126	135
1930	136	131	113	112
1931	119	97	109	131
1932	168	104	123	143
1933	148	142	131	135
1934	169	176	140	154
1935	169	159	141	172
1936	182	183	157	173
1937	149	156	139	167
1938	189	129	105	138

TABLE 1.15 : QUARTERLY INDEX OF PRODUCTION (LONDON & CAMBRIDGE) : TOTAL (1924 AVERAGE = 100)

	MAR	JUN	SEP	DEC
1920	120.2	114.2	115.3	105.1
1921	89.6	54.4	86.7	86.6
1922	85.9	88.3	94.8	93.5
1923	98.4	97.7	91.9	102.8
1924	98.8	99.9	97.9	103.8
1925	102.6	98.2	90.1	99.1
1926	102.2	72.0	57.3	69.7
1927	110.8	108.1	105.9	107.4
1928	105.7	103.7	95.4	105.2
1929	108.3	111.0	108.2	114.8
1930	109.6	100.9	90.7	92.7
1931	85.1	80.6	81.1	90.5
1932	91.3	83.2	77.8	87.2
1933	88.0	88.8	87.9	97.4
1934	102.5	102.6	96.8	105.2
1935	104.0	108.4	104.5	116.5
1936	116.3	118.4	114.6	122.2
1937	119.6	126.5	121.3	128.7
1938	122.8	108.1	99.3	108.8

TABLE 1.16 : QUARTERLY INDEX OF PRODUCTION (LONDON & CAMBRIDGE) : TOTAL SEASONALLY ADJUSTED(1924 AVERAGE = 100)

	MAR	JUN	SEP	DEC
1920	116	117	120	102
1921	86	56	90	84
1922	83	90	99	91
1923	95	100	96	100
1924	95	102	102	101
1925	99	100	94	97
1926	98	74	60	68
1927	107	111	110	105
1928	102	106	99	103
1929	104	114	113	112
1930	106	103	94	90
1931	82	82	84	88
1932	88	85	81	85
1933	85	91	92	95
1934	99	105	101	103
1935	100	111	109	114
1936	112	121	119	119
1937	115	129	126	125
1938	118	111	103	106

TABLE 1.17 : BOARD OF TRADE INDEX OF INDUSTRIAL PRODUCTION : GROUP 1
(1924 AVERAGE = 100)

	MAR	JUN	SEP	DEC
1928	96.2	85.5	83.2	91.9
1929	94.4	92.6	94.4	100.8
1930	102.0	87.4	84.3	91.4
1931	85.3	79.7	75.7	85.6
1932	83.0	77.3	68.8	80.8
1933	83.0	71.5	70.2	82.8
1934	80.9	71.5	69.9	78.4
1935	78.9	72.3	71.0	81.2
1936	83.3	73.3	74.3	81.9
1937	82.3	83.2	79.2	86.0
1938	86.1	73.9	71.2	79.8
1939	83.2	77.8		

TABLE 1.18 : BOARD OF TRADE INDEX OF INDUSTRIAL PRODUCTION : GROUP 1
SEASONALLY ADJUSTED (1924 AVERAGE = 100)

	MAR	JUN	SEP	DEC
1928	91	89	89	87
1929	90	96	101	96
1930	97	91	90	87
1931	81	83	81	81
1932	79	80	73	77
1933	79	74	75	79
1934	77	74	75	75
1935	75	75	76	77
1936	79	76	79	78
1937	78	87	85	82
1938	82	77	76	76
1939	79	81		

TABLE 1.19 : BOARD OF TRADE INDEX OF INDUSTRIAL PRODUCTION : GROUP 2
(1924 AVERAGE = 100)

	MAR	JUN	SEP	DEC
1928	105.6	100.9	97.4	105.2
1929	112.4	117.8	113.7	112.2
1930	113.8	95.5	80.0	65.8
1931	68.0	62.9	61.0	71.6
1932	70.4	66.6	61.5	66.2
1933	72.3	78.5	84.2	93.7
1934	121.2	120.7	113.5	119.4
1935	125.1	126.4	127.3	136.8
1936	150.0	153.4	153.0	159.6
1937	162.2	169.9	169.8	181.9
1938	172.8	135.0	109.2	122.9
1939	153.0	181.1		

TABLE 1.20 : BOARD OF TRADE INDEX OF INDUSTRIAL PRODUCTION : GROUP 2
SEASONALLY ADJUSTED (1924 AVERAGE = 100)

	MAR	JUN	SEP	DEC
1928	101	101	101	106
1929	108	117	118	113
1930	109	95	83	66
1931	65	63	64	72
1932	67	66	64	67
1933	69	78	88	94
1934	116	120	118	120
1935	120	126	133	138
1936	144	153	159	161
1937	155	169	177	183
1938	166	135	114	124
1939	147	181		

TABLE 1.21 : BOARD OF TRADE INDEX OF INDUSTRIAL PRODUCTION : GROUP 3
(1924 AVERAGE = 100)

	MAR	JUN	SEP	DEC
1928	121.6	125.7	109.9	119.8
1929	115.7	128.7	114.6	123.0
1930	105.7	123.7	128.6	118.3
1931	95.5	110.9	96.7	97.4
1932	97.8	93.4	94.2	99.8
1933	81.9	104.5	100.3	120.7
1934	155.1	168.0	189.2	215.8
1935	211.0	205.4	202.7	196.0
1936	200.0	209.1	215.6	228.5
1937	229.1	247.4	257.8	246.6
1938	227.5	218.7	211.9	209.8
1939	207.3	233.0		

TABLE 1.22 : BOARD OF TRADE INDEX OF INDUSTRIAL PRODUCTION : GROUP 3
SEASONALLY ADJUSTED (1924 AVERAGE = 100)

	MAR	JUN	SEP	DEC
1928	126	123	111	117
1929	120	126	115	121
1930	110	121	130	116
1931	99	108	97	95
1932	101	91	95	98
1933	85	102	101	118
1934	161	164	191	212
1935	219	201	204	192
1936	207	204	217	224
1937	237	242	260	242
1938	236	214	214	206
1939	215	228		

TABLE 1.23 : BOARD OF TRADE INDEX OF INDUSTRIAL PRODUCTION : GROUP 4
(1924 AVERAGE = 100)

	MAR	JUN	SEP	DEC
1928	117.2	116.2	107.9	111.2
1929	120.0	124.7	119.3	120.0
1930	125.5	122.6	112.2	105.9
1931	102.5	98.7	89.2	89.1
1932	90.7	90.4	84.9	88.2
1933	93.0	97.0	93.5	100.4
1934	99.4	103.4	103.6	114.7
1935	118.3	116.0	114.5	121.0
1936	130.4	137.3	136.4	148.4
1937	152.8	154.9	151.2	151.6
1938	148.7	144.3	139.6	145.1
1939	149.3	153.2		

TABLE 1.24 : BOARD OF TRADE INDEX OF INDUSTRIAL PRODUCTION : GROUP 4
SEASONALLY ADJUSTED (1924 AVERAGE = 100)

	MAR	JUN	SEP	DEC
1928	115	114	111	112
1929	118	123	123	120
1930	123	120	116	106
1931	101	97	92	89
1932	89	89	88	89
1933	91	95	96	101
1934	98	102	107	115
1935	116	114	118	121
1936	128	135	141	149
1937	150	152	156	152
1938	146	142	144	146
1939	146	151		

TABLE 1.25 : BOARD OF TRADE INDEX OF INDUSTRIAL PRODUCTION : GROUP 5
(1930 AVERAGE = 100)

	MAR	JUN	SEP	DEC
1934	123.2	136.3	143.6	138.1
1935	135.9	148.5	153.5	150.2
1936	148.8	157.8	164.7	157.3
1937	148.5	155.9	160.3	148.3
1938	146.1	152.5	148.0	134.8
1939	126.7	137.6		

TABLE 1.26 : BOARD OF TRADE INDEX OF INDUSTRIAL PRODUCTION : GROUP 5
SEASONALLY ADJUSTED (1924 AVERAGE = 100)

	MAR	JUN	SEP	DEC
1934	129	134	138	140
1935	142	146	147	152
1936	155	155	158	160
1937	155	153	154	150
1938	153	150	142	137
1939	132	135		

TABLE 1.27 : BOARD OF TRADE INDEX OF INDUSTRIAL PRODUCTION : GROUP 6
(1924 AVERAGE = 100)

	MAR	JUN	SEP	DEC
1928	106.9	99.5	91.9	101.2
1929	102.0	99.8	91.4	100.7
1930	92.4	78.2	71.4	75.8
1931	72.6	75.0	70.7	89.6
1932	91.1	86.9	76.1	86.2
1933	87.6	86.9	88.8	95.9
1934	108.9	102.3	98.5	107.4
1935	109.4	107.4	104.2	116.4
1936	117.1	114.9	113.3	119.8
1937	119.7	124.3	117.3	115.7
1938	107.5	97.9	98.0	104.9
1939	111.0	116.2		

TABLE 1.28 : BOARD OF TRADE INDEX OF INDUSTRIAL PRODUCTION : GROUP 6
SEASONALLY ADJUSTED (1924 AVERAGE = 100)

	MAR	JUN	SEP	DEC
1928	104	100	98	98
1929	99	100	97	97
1930	90	79	76	73
1931	70	76	75	87
1932	88	87	81	83
1933	85	87	94	93
1934	106	103	105	104
1935	106	108	111	113
1936	114	116	120	116
1937	116	125	125	112
1938	104	99	104	102
1939	107	117		

TABLE 1.29 : BOARD OF TRADE INDEX OF INDUSTRIAL PRODUCTION : GROUP 7
(1924 AVERAGE = 100)

	MAR	JUN	SEP	DEC
1928	110.5	109.4	106.3	115.1
1929	108.3	114.6	120.3	119.8
1930	106.3	102.4	105.5	94.6
1931	96.1	94.4	90.7	99.4
1932	101.3	102.8	92.5	95.7
1933	96.7	101.3	99.8	106.0
1934	112.4	110.4	108.0	110.8
1935	114.0	113.4	113.6	125.5
1936	123.2	119.1	125.7	127.2
1937	129.0	133.4	130.6	132.4
1938	128.4	119.1	117.0	126.1
1939	128.4	138.4		

TABLE 1.30 : BOARD OF TRADE INDEX OF INDUSTRIAL PRODUCTION : GROUP 7
SEASONALLY ADJUSTED (1924 AVERAGE = 100)

	MAR	JUN	SEP	DEC
1928	110	110	108	114
1929	108	115	122	118
1930	106	103	107	93
1931	96	95	92	98
1932	101	103	94	94
1933	96	102	101	105
1934	112	111	109	109
1935	114	114	115	124
1936	123	119	127	125
1937	129	134	132	131
1938	128	119	119	124
1939	128	138		

TABLE 1.31 : BOARD OF TRADE INDEX OF INDUSTRIAL PRODUCTION : GROUP 8
(1924 AVERAGE = 100)

	MAR	JUN	SEP	DEC
1928	120.0	105.8	90.9	91.4
1929	100.3	100.7	95.2	97.9
1930	108.5	103.8	98.3	95.0
1931	101.3	99.1	95.4	101.3
1932	99.6	96.6	93.3	96.1
1933	103.3	114.2	105.5	101.7
1934	116.5	111.4	102.1	113.7
1935	124.0	122.3	116.5	129.6
1936	134.0	128.5	123.6	127.0
1937	121.2	121.7	117.4	115.1
1938	118.5	108.5	104.0	114.0
1939	126.6	121.5		

TABLE 1.32 : BOARD OF TRADE INDEX OF INDUSTRIAL PRODUCTION : GROUP 8
SEASONALLY ADJUSTED (1924 AVERAGE = 100)

	MAR	JUN	SEP	DEC
1928	115	104	95	93
1929	97	99	99	99
1930	104	102	103	96
1931	97	97	100	103
1932	96	95	97	98
1933	99	112	110	103
1934	112	110	106	115
1935	119	120	122	132
1936	129	126	129	129
1937	117	120	122	117
1938	114	107	108	116
1939	122	120		

TABLE 1.33 : BOARD OF TRADE INDEX OF INDUSTRIAL PRODUCTION : GROUP 9
(1924 AVERAGE = 100)

	MAR	JUN	SEP	DEC
1928	98.7	99.3	105.1	104.8
1929	97.5	109.0	111.8	105.7
1930	96.9	104.9	108.3	109.4
1931	99.0	101.9	108.5	105.2
1932	94.1	101.7	97.9	96.5
1933	89.2	102.3	102.5	102.7
1934	101.0	107.3	106.1	112.3
1935	103.4	113.7	114.4	119.3
1936	112.0	119.9	120.6	126.9
1937	116.5	130.8	126.0	129.0
1938	121.5	129.3	128.5	129.2
1939	125.2	135.4		

TABLE 1.34 : BOARD OF TRADE INDEX OF INDUSTRIAL PRODUCTION : GROUP 9
SEASONALLY ADJUSTED (1924 AVERAGE = 100)

	MAR	JUN	SEP	DEC
1928	105	98	103	103
1929	104	107	110	103
1930	103	103	106	107
1931	105	100	106	103
1932	100	100	96	94
1933	95	100	101	101
1934	107	105	104	110
1935	110	112	112	117
1936	119	118	118	124
1937	124	128	124	126
1938	129	127	126	126
1939	133	133		

TABLE 1.35 : BOARD OF TRADE INDEX OF INDUSTRIAL PRODUCTION : TOTAL (1924 AVERAGE = 100)

	MAR	JUN	SEP	DEC
1928	109.3	103.6	100.2	108.4
1929	110.6	112.0	110.7	114.0
1930	111.0	103.1	99.5	99.0
1931	94.6	92.1	89.3	97.3
1932	95.0	94.3	87.4	95.0
1933	94.8	96.7	96.8	105.0
1934	117.0	115.7	114.2	123.8
1935	125.0	123.4	122.5	133.6
1936	136.3	136.7	135.5	146.3
1937	145.1	147.8	144.0	150.9
1938	146.2	134.7	129.5	139.4
1939	145.0	147.6		

TABLE 1.36 : BOARD OF TRADE INDEX OF INDUSTRIAL PRODUCTION : TOTAL SEASONALLY ADJUSTED (1924 AVERAGE = 100)

	MAR	JUN	SEP	DEC
1928	107	104	104	106
1929	109	113	115	112
1930	109	104	103	97
1931	93	93	93	95
1932	93	95	91	93
1933	93	97	100	103
1934	115	116	118	121
1935	123	124	127	131
1936	134	137	140	143
1937	143	149	149	148
1938	144	135	134	136
1939	143	148		

2 Prices and Retail Sales

TABLES

SOURCES

Tables 2.1–2.6 *Board of Trade Journal*
Tables 2.7–2.12 *The Statist*
Tables 2.13–2.16 *Ministry of Labour Gazette*
Tables 2.17–2.22 *Board of Trade Journal*

There are eight basic series of monthly prices in this collection, six wholesale and two retail; three are taken from the Board of Trade source, two from the *Ministry of Labour Gazette* and three from *The Statist*. Also included in this section is an index of retail sales sub-divided into an index for sales of food and perishables, and one for other merchandise.

The Board of Trade wholesale price index was published around the eighth of each month. The index was the geometric mean of the present age price changes from the base of a large number of commodities. After 1935, 200 commodities were used, prior to that there had been 150 in the list. As wide a range of products as possible was aimed for and the index is made up of the main raw materials, semi-manufactured goods and fully finished articles. Clearly an index number of wholesale prices cannot be representative of goods in all stages of manufacture, and the commodities were taken as close to that 'final' stage as possible. The commodities were weighted according to relative size as indicated by the most recent census of production. The 1907 census was used initially and the weightings were revised with the changed importance shown by each subsequent census of production and Trade Accounts data. That is, the weights used were proportional to the total value of goods produced, together with the value of imports passing directly into consumption. The weights were taken from the most recent census of production. The price quotations used were mostly from published journals but in a few cases the Board of Trade secured further quotations for which published particulars were not regularly available. The prices for dutiable goods are inclusive of the appropriate amount of the duty, and represent the position after the payment of subsidies. An extensive and detailed account of the commodities, method of construction and final results was published by the Board of Trade in 1935.[1] Each month, figures were also given for the following eleven sub-groups: cereals; meat, fish and eggs; other food and tobacco; coal; iron and steel; non-ferrous metals; cotton; wool; other textiles; chemicals and oils; miscellaneous. The sum of the first three of these groups makes up the total food index and the remainder comprise the total materials index, again weighted by the method described.

Sauerbeck first presented his index to the Royal Statistical

Society in 1886. The base period was 1866–77. From 1912 onwards *The Statist* continued the index in slightly modified form and it later acquired the full name of Sauerbeck–Statist index. The index numbers were obtained by expressing current wholesale prices of nineteen foodstuffs and twenty-six raw materials toward the end of each month, as percentages of their prices in the base period. *The Statist* revised the base to 1913. The relative importance of different classes of commodities within food and raw materials was allowed for in an approximate way in the number of price series included in each class: vegetable foods (eight); animal foods (seven); miscellaneous foods (four); minerals (seven); textiles (eight); miscellaneous products (eleven).

None of the above indices measures the movements in retail prices, which is why two indices from the Ministry of Labour have been included, the retail price index for food and a total retail price index. The official cost-of-living index was instituted at the beginning of the First World War for the purpose of tracking what had happened to the standard of living of most people. It was therefore based on a wide selection of the principal items of working-class family expenditure. The items included fell under five headings: food, rent, clothing, fuel and light, others. In all cases they were retail prices collected, where possible, from hundreds of retail outlets across the country and quite distinct from those used by the Board of Trade for the wholesale price index. The only change of significance was the dropping of sources of information in the Irish Free State after April 1923. The items included under each heading were as follows:

1 *Food* beef, mutton, bacon, fish, flour, bread, potatoes, tea, sugar, milk, butter, margarine, cheese, eggs. (The most important omissions were fruit and vegetables.)

2 *Rent* of unfurnished dwellings. After 1928 'decontrolled' rents were included.

3 *Clothing* men's suits, overcoats, woollen and cotton materials, underclothing, hosiery, boots and shoes.

4 *Fuel and Light* coal, gas, lamp oil, candles, matches.

5 *Other* soap, soda, domestic ironmongery, brushes, pottery, tobacco and cigarettes, fares, newspapers.

The weights used in the compilation of the index were based on the average expenditure shown by 1,944 working-class family budgets collected in 1904, and one of the criticisms this index has attracted has been that the list of items of which account was taken and the weights used were both in need of revision even as an index of working-class expenditure by as early as the 1920s. The chief deficiency of course is that it was designed to cover only working-class expenditure and must be regarded as less than an ideal guide to the movement in retail prices generally.

Some guide to retail sales can be obtained, though only for short periods. The series published by the Board of Trade were obtained from returns made to the Bank of England and were built up from average daily sales.[2] Tables 2.17–2.22 present the available data.

NOTES

1 *Board of Trade Journal*, 24 January 1935. Sir Alfred Flux was the statistician responsible for the production of the Board of Trade index and in two papers presented to the Royal Statistical Society he set out the aims and methods: A. W. Flux, 'The measurement of price changes', *JRSS*, LXXXIV, Part II (1921); and 'The measurement of price changes: retrospect and prospect', *JRSS*, XCVI, Part IV (1933).

2 Further details can be obtained in several special articles in the *Board of Trade Journal*: 15 March 1934, p. 397; 28 February 1935, p. 320; 9 February 1939, p. 211.

TABLE 2.1 : BOARD OF TRADE WHOLESALE PRICE INDEX : GENERAL
(1924 AVERAGE = 100)

	JAN	FEB	MAR	APR	MAY	JUN	JUL	AUG	SEP	OCT	NOV	DEC
1919	148.1	148.7	152.3	151.1	142.1	143.3	145.7	154.7	159.5	167.4	174.0	178.8
1920	178.8	186.6	192.0	195.7	195.7	193.8	190.8	188.4	187.2	181.8	172.8	158.9
1921	148.1	135.5	127.0	123.4	121.6	119.2	116.8	114.4	112.6	109.0	104.2	101.1
1922	98.7	97.5	96.3	96.3	96.3	96.3	96.3	93.9	92.7	93.3	94.5	93.9
1923	94.5	95.1	96.3	96.9	96.3	95.7	94.5	93.3	95.1	95.1	96.9	98.7
1924	99.3	100.5	99.3	99.3	98.7	98.1	98.1	99.3	100.5	102.3	102.3	102.3
1925	102.9	101.7	99.9	97.5	95.7	94.5	94.5	93.9	93.3	92.7	92.1	91.5
1926	90.3	89.1	86.7	86.7	87.3	87.9	89.7	89.7	90.9	91.5	91.5	87.9
1927	86.7	86.1	84.9	84.3	84.9	85.5	84.9	84.9	85.5	84.9	84.9	84.3
1928	84.9	84.3	84.9	86.1	86.7	86.1	84.9	83.7	83.1	83.1	83.1	83.1
1929	83.2	83.3	84.4	83.4	81.7	81.6	82.7	81.8	81.7	81.9	80.6	79.7
1930	78.8	76.9	74.9	74.4	73.3	72.6	71.7	70.9	69.5	68.0	67.4	65.5
1931	64.3	63.9	63.7	63.6	62.8	62.1	61.5	59.9	59.7	62.8	64.0	63.7
1932	63.4	63.4	63.0	61.6	60.6	58.9	58.8	59.9	61.4	60.8	60.8	60.8
1933	60.3	59.5	58.7	58.5	59.7	61.2	61.5	61.7	62.0	61.8	61.9	61.9
1934	63.8	64.1	63.4	63.1	62.7	63.2	62.8	64.0	63.6	63.1	62.9	63.1
1935	63.5	63.3	62.5	62.9	63.5	63.6	63.3	63.6	64.4	65.6	65.7	65.8
1936	66.0	65.9	65.9	66.1	66.1	66.6	67.3	68.5	69.1	70.2	70.7	72.5
1937	74.0	74.7	77.2	78.2	79.6	79.6	80.2	80.1	79.9	79.5	78.0	77.4
1938	77.5	76.1	74.8	74.1	73.4	72.4	72.3	71.5	70.7	71.2	70.7	70.6
1939	69.9	69.6	69.4	69.9	70.3	70.5	70.6	70.6	75.9	79.7	84.3	86.9

TABLE 2.2 : BOARD OF TRADE WHOLESALE PRICE INDEX : GENERAL.
SEASONALLY ADJUSTED (1924 AVERAGE = 100)

	JAN	FEB	MAR	APR	MAY	JUN	JUL	AUG	SEP	OCT	NOV	DEC
1919	148	149	153	152	142	144	148	156	159	165	172	177
1920	179	187	193	196	196	194	193	190	186	180	170	158
1921	148	136	128	124	122	120	118	115	112	108	103	100
1922	99	98	97	97	97	97	98	95	92	92	93	93
1923	95	95	97	97	97	96	96	94	95	94	96	98
1924	99	101	100	100	99	98	99	100	100	101	101	102
1925	103	102	101	98	96	95	96	95	93	92	91	91
1926	90	89	87	87	88	88	90	90	91	91	90	88
1927	87	86	85	85	85	86	85	85	85	84	84	84
1928	85	84	85	86	87	87	85	84	83	82	82	83
1929	83	83	85	84	82	82	83	82	82	81	80	79
1930	79	77	75	75	74	73	72	71	69	67	67	65
1931	64	64	64	64	63	63	62	60	60	62	63	63
1932	63	63	63	62	61	59	59	60	61	60	60	61
1933	60	59	59	59	60	61	61	61	62	61	62	62
1934	63	64	64	64	63	63	63	64	63	63	63	63
1935	63	63	63	63	64	64	63	63	64	65	66	66
1936	65	66	66	67	66	67	67	68	69	70	71	72
1937	73	75	78	79	80	80	80	80	80	79	78	77
1938	77	76	75	75	74	73	72	71	70	71	71	71
1939	69	70	70	70	71	71	71	70	76	79	84	87

TABLE 2.3 : BOARD OF TRADE WHOLESALE PRICE INDEX : FOOD
(1924 AVERAGE = 100)

	JAN	FEB	MAR	APR	MAY	JUN	JUL	AUG	SEP	OCT	NOV	DEC
1920	153.8	153.8	159.3	165.3	164.1	166.5	167.1	165.3	165.3	170.1	168.9	162.3
1921	154.4	140.6	137.0	134.0	129.8	128.0	126.2	126.2	119.6	110.0	106.4	104.0
1922	101.6	104.6	102.8	103.4	103.4	101.6	101.6	96.2	93.8	94.4	96.2	93.8
1923	94.4	91.9	90.7	89.5	90.1	91.9	93.1	91.9	95.6	96.2	95.6	96.2
1924	98.6	100.4	97.4	95.0	95.6	95.6	96.2	99.2	102.8	107.6	106.4	105.8
1925	107.8	105.9	103.2	101.5	100.5	99.8	98.8	98.4	97.6	96.6	97.1	98.0
1926	95.2	93.1	90.0	91.2	94.8	93.3	93.0	92.6	91.9	94.3	94.2	93.2
1927	92.3	91.6	88.4	89.1	91.9	93.9	92.4	90.9	92.2	91.7	91.4	90.8
1928	92.1	91.1	91.4	95.4	95.8	94.7	91.9	90.7	88.7	89.2	89.3	89.1
1929	88.7	89.4	90.3	88.5	86.3	86.2	89.4	86.8	85.8	87.2	85.6	84.6
1930	83.4	81.0	77.7	77.6	76.5	76.6	76.4	75.9	74.4	72.9	72.5	69.8
1931	68.1	67.1	66.6	67.4	67.8	67.7	65.5	64.6	64.7	67.7	69.1	68.0
1932	69.0	68.7	69.5	69.2	68.8	66.8	64.9	64.5	64.6	63.6	64.0	64.8
1933	64.1	62.8	61.4	60.6	61.4	62.3	61.0	62.3	63.1	62.4	62.5	61.9
1934	62.8	62.5	60.6	59.8	60.1	62.3	62.4	66.5	66.1	64.6	64.5	64.5
1935	66.2	65.9	64.3	64.9	65.5	65.9	64.7	65.3	67.0	68.1	67.2	67.4
1936	67.7	67.1	66.4	66.4	67.1	68.0	68.4	71.3	72.3	74.6	73.6	75.6
1937	75.6	75.0	76.6	77.6	77.5	77.3	78.3	78.2	78.9	80.2	79.5	79.5
1938	79.9	78.7	76.6	76.3	76.4	75.6	74.4	72.1	69.9	70.5	69.0	69.8
1939	70.4	69.3	68.5	69.6	69.9	69.9	69.5	68.8	77.0	83.2	86.5	89.9

TABLE 2.4 : BOARD OF TRADE WHOLESALE PRICE INDEX : FOOD.
SEASONALLY ADJUSTED (1924 AVERAGE = 100)

	JAN	FEB	MAR	APR	MAY	JUN	JUL	AUG	SEP	OCT	NOV	DEC
1920	152	154	162	169	166	168	167	165	164	168	166	161
1921	153	141	139	137	131	129	126	126	119	109	105	103
1922	101	105	105	105	104	102	101	96	93	93	95	93
1923	94	92	92	91	91	93	93	92	95	95	94	95
1924	98	101	99	97	97	96	96	99	102	106	105	105
1925	107	106	105	103	101	101	99	98	97	95	96	97
1926	94	93	92	93	96	94	93	93	93	94	93	93
1927	92	92	89	89	92	93	92	92	93	91	91	91
1928	92	91	92	96	95	94	92	91	89	89	89	89
1929	88	90	91	89	86	86	89	87	87	87	85	84
1930	83	81	79	78	76	76	76	76	75	73	72	70
1931	68	67	67	68	68	67	65	65	65	67	69	68
1932	69	69	70	69	69	66	65	65	65	63	63	65
1933	64	63	62	61	61	62	62	62	63	62	62	62
1934	62	62	61	61	61	63	63	66	65	64	64	64
1935	65	66	65	66	66	67	65	65	66	67	67	67
1936	67	67	67	67	68	69	69	71	72	74	73	75
1937	75	75	78	79	78	78	79	78	78	79	79	79
1938	79	78	78	77	77	76	75	72	69	70	69	69
1939	69	69	69	70	71	71	70	68	76	82	86	89

TABLE 2.5 : BOARD OF TRADE WHOLESALE PRICE INDEX : MATERIALS
(1924 AVERAGE = 100)

	JAN	FEB	MAR	APR	MAY	JUN	JUL	AUG	SEP	OCT	NOV	DEC
1920	194.2	208.1	212.9	214.7	214.7	211.1	205.1	202.7	200.8	188.8	174.9	157.4
1921	144.8	133.3	121.8	117.6	117.0	114.6	112.2	108.6	109.2	108.6	103.1	99.5
1922	97.1	94.1	92.9	92.9	93.5	93.5	93.5	92.9	92.3	92.9	94.1	93.5
1923	94.7	96.5	100.1	101.9	100.1	98.3	95.3	94.1	94.7	94.7	97.7	99.5
1924	100.1	100.7	100.7	101.3	100.1	98.9	98.9	99.5	99.5	99.5	100.1	100.7
1925	100.4	99.4	98.4	95.8	93.1	91.9	92.1	91.6	91.0	90.4	89.1	88.1
1926	87.6	86.5	84.9	83.9	83.2	85.3	87.9	88.8	90.2	90.0	90.4	85.1
1927	83.3	82.7	82.6	81.5	81.3	80.9	81.1	81.7	82.1	81.7	81.6	81.1
1928	81.3	80.9	81.1	81.3	81.6	81.3	81.3	80.3	79.8	79.9	79.7	80.0
1929	80.3	80.0	81.2	80.7	79.3	79.1	79.2	79.1	79.5	79.1	78.0	77.1
1930	76.3	74.7	73.4	72.6	71.5	70.4	69.2	68.2	67.0	65.4	64.7	63.3
1931	62.4	62.1	62.1	61.5	60.1	59.1	59.2	57.3	57.0	60.2	61.4	61.5
1932	61.0	60.7	59.7	57.8	56.5	55.0	55.7	57.6	59.7	59.3	59.1	58.7
1933	58.4	57.8	57.4	57.3	58.8	60.6	61.8	61.3	61.4	61.4	61.5	61.8
1934	63.1	63.9	63.5	63.1	62.5	62.4	62.2	62.0	61.9	61.7	61.7	62.0
1935	62.0	61.8	61.3	61.7	62.3	62.2	62.5	62.5	62.9	64.0	64.6	64.7
1936	65.0	65.2	65.4	65.6	65.3	65.6	66.5	66.8	67.3	67.7	69.0	70.7
1937	72.8	74.2	77.1	78.3	80.3	80.3	80.8	80.7	80.2	78.8	76.9	76.0
1938	75.9	74.4	73.6	72.7	71.5	70.5	70.9	70.9	70.8	71.3	71.4	70.8
1939	69.3	69.4	69.6	69.7	70.2	70.5	70.8	71.1	74.9	77.5	84.1	86.5

TABLE 2.6 : BOARD OF TRADE WHOLESALE PRICE INDEX : MATERIALS.
SEASONALLY ADJUSTED (1924 AVERAGE = 100)

	JAN	FEB	MAR	APR	MAY	JUN	JUL	AUG	SEP	OCT	NOV	DEC
1920	194	210	216	217	217	213	205	202	198	186	173	157
1921	145	134	123	119	118	116	112	108	108	107	102	99
1922	97	95	94	94	95	94	93	93	91	91	93	93
1923	95	97	101	103	101	99	95	94	93	93	96	99
1924	100	101	102	102	101	100	99	99	98	98	99	100
1925	100	100	100	97	94	93	92	91	90	89	88	88
1926	88	87	86	85	84	86	88	89	90	89	89	85
1927	83	83	83	82	82	82	82	82	82	81	80	81
1928	81	81	81	82	82	82	82	81	79	79	78	80
1929	80	80	81	81	80	80	80	79	79	78	77	77
1930	76	75	73	73	72	71	70	68	67	65	64	63
1931	62	62	62	62	61	60	60	57	57	59	60	61
1932	61	61	60	58	57	56	56	58	59	59	58	58
1933	58	58	57	58	59	61	61	61	61	61	62	62
1934	63	64	63	63	63	63	62	62	62	62	62	62
1935	62	62	61	62	62	63	62	62	63	64	65	65
1936	65	65	65	66	65	66	66	67	67	68	69	71
1937	73	74	77	78	80	81	80	81	80	79	77	76
1938	76	74	73	73	72	71	70	71	71	71	72	71
1939	69	69	69	70	70	71	70	71	75	78	84	87

TABLE 2.7 : SAUERBECK-STATIST WHOLESALE PRICE INDEX : TOTAL
(1924 AVERAGE = 100)

	JAN	FEB	MAR	APR	MAY	JUN	JUL	AUG	SEP	OCT	NOV	DEC
1919	139.3	135.9	133.8	141.1	144.6	149.6	154.2	155.7	162.6	167.5	170.5	149.4
1920	177.8	188.8	189.8	192.9	188.5	185.4	184.6	183.8	180.3	173.9	162.3	150.2
1921	143.0	132.7	128.5	123.1	117.6	113.0	114.7	111.9	108.3	100.3	99.1	96.9
1922	96.1	95.8	96.6	97.7	98.2	98.3	97.2	94.0	92.7	94.3	94.7	93.6
1923	94.4	95.6	96.2	97.2	95.8	92.7	90.5	90.6	92.7	92.6	96.0	96.6
1924	98.1	99.1	97.8	97.7	97.4	97.4	99.0	98.8	101.0	104.4	104.0	105.8
1925	103.2	102.0	100.2	98.3	97.1	93.5	95.9	95.9	94.7	92.9	94.7	92.9
1926	92.3	91.1	89.8	89.8	89.8	89.2	89.8	90.4	91.7	93.5	93.5	88.6
1927	88.0	88.6	88.0	88.0	88.6	88.0	87.4	88.0	86.8	86.2	86.8	86.8
1928	86.2	86.2	88.0	89.8	90.4	87.4	85.6	84.4	83.2	83.2	83.8	83.8
1929	84.0	86.0	87.0	84.0	81.0	81.0	83.0	82.0	81.0	80.0	78.0	78.5
1930	77.0	75.0	74.0	73.0	71.0	69.0	68.0	66.0	65.0	65.0	64.0	62.5
1931	61.5	61.5	61.5	61.0	59.0	59.5	57.5	57.0	58.0	59.0	60.0	61.5
1932	61.0	62.5	60.5	59.5	57.5	55.5	57.0	58.0	58.0	56.0	56.0	56.0
1933	56.0	55.5	55.5	56.5	58.0	58.5	59.0	58.5	58.0	58.0	57.0	57.5
1934	59.5	59.5	59.0	58.5	58.5	58.0	59.5	60.0	59.0	58.5	58.5	59.5
1935	60.0	60.0	59.5	60.5	61.5	60.0	60.5	60.5	61.0	61.5	62.0	62.5
1936	62.5	62.5	62.0	61.5	61.5	60.5	62.5	64.0	65.0	66.0	68.0	71.0
1937	71.5	73.0	77.0	75.0	76.0	75.0	76.0	75.0	74.0	72.0	69.5	70.0
1938	69.5	69.5	68.0	67.0	65.5	65.5	65.5	63.5	63.5	64.0	63.0	64.0
1939	64.0	63.5	64.0	65.0	65.0	65.0	64.0	65.0	72.0	76.0	81.0	86.5

TABLE 2.8 : SAUERBECK-STATIST WHOLESALE PRICE INDEX : TOTAL
SEASONALLY ADJUSTED (1924 AVERAGE = 100)

	JAN	FEB	MAR	APR	MAY	JUN	JUL	AUG	SEP	OCT	NOV	DEC
1919	139	135	133	140	145	151	154	156	163	168	171	150
1920	177	188	188	192	188	187	185	184	180	174	162	151
1921	143	132	128	122	118	114	115	112	108	100	99	97
1922	96	95	96	97	98	99	97	94	93	94	95	94
1923	94	95	96	97	96	94	90	91	93	93	96	97
1924	98	99	98	98	98	99	99	99	101	105	105	107
1925	103	101	100	98	97	95	96	96	95	93	95	93
1926	92	91	89	89	90	90	90	91	92	94	94	89
1927	88	88	87	87	89	89	87	88	87	86	87	87
1928	86	86	87	89	90	88	86	85	83	83	84	84
1929	84	85	86	83	81	82	83	82	81	80	78	79
1930	77	75	73	73	71	70	68	66	65	65	64	63
1931	61	61	61	61	59	60	57	57	58	59	60	62
1932	61	62	60	59	57	56	57	58	58	56	56	56
1933	56	55	55	56	58	59	59	59	58	58	57	58
1934	59	59	59	58	58	59	59	60	59	59	59	60
1935	60	60	59	60	61	61	60	61	61	62	62	63
1936	62	62	62	61	61	61	62	64	65	66	68	71
1937	71	73	76	75	76	76	76	75	74	72	70	70
1938	69	69	68	67	65	66	65	64	64	64	63	64
1939	64	63	64	65	65	66	64	65	72	76	81	87

TABLE 2.9 : SAUERBECK-STATIST WHOLESALE PRICE INDEX : FOOD
(1924 AVERAGE = 100)

	JAN	FEB	MAR	APR	MAY	JUN	JUL	AUG	SEP	OCT	NOV	DEC
1919	138.1	138.7	131.6	131.6	133.4	135.2	136.4	142.9	144.0	149.4	152.3	153.5
1920	156.4	168.8	177.1	186.0	187.7	191.9	191.9	188.3	181.8	178.3	171.8	149.4
1921	148.2	138.1	137.0	132.8	124.6	122.2	121.6	122.2	112.2	99.2	99.2	94.5
1922	95.6	98.0	102.7	108.0	105.7	105.1	102.7	97.4	93.3	95.0	95.6	96.2
1923	95.0	96.2	96.2	97.4	96.2	90.9	91.5	91.5	93.9	91.5	92.7	92.7
1924	98.0	97.4	94.5	96.8	97.4	98.0	98.0	99.8	102.7	106.8	103.9	106.8
1925	107.0	105.0	103.0	101.0	101.0	94.0	96.0	98.0	94.0	92.0	93.0	93.0
1926	92.0	91.0	89.0	92.0	92.0	93.0	93.0	93.0	92.0	90.0	90.0	91.0
1927	90.0	89.0	89.0	91.0	92.0	90.0	87.0	88.0	86.0	83.0	85.0	86.0
1928	86.0	89.0	93.0	94.0	97.0	92.0	88.0	85.0	84.0	84.0	85.0	85.0
1929	85.0	87.0	86.0	86.0	82.5	83.5	86.0	84.5	83.0	82.5	80.0	81.0
1930	80.5	79.0	76.0	77.0	73.0	72.5	72.0	69.5	70.0	70.0	68.0	67.5
1931	67.5	65.5	66.0	66.5	65.0	65.0	63.0	62.0	63.0	63.0	63.0	65.5
1932	64.5	67.0	65.5	66.0	65.5	59.5	61.0	59.5	59.5	56.5	56.0	56.5
1933	57.5	57.0	57.5	58.0	57.5	57.0	58.0	58.0	57.5	57.0	56.0	57.0
1934	59.5	59.5	58.0	58.0	59.0	59.0	62.0	63.0	60.5	59.5	58.5	60.0
1935	59.5	59.0	58.0	59.0	60.0	58.5	58.5	59.0	59.5	59.5	58.5	59.5
1936	60.5	59.5	59.0	59.5	60.0	60.0	61.0	63.0	64.0	65.5	65.5	67.5
1937	67.5	68.5	73.0	73.0	73.5	72.0	73.0	72.5	72.5	72.5	70.5	71.5
1938	70.5	70.0	69.0	69.0	68.0	67.5	65.0	62.0	61.0	59.5	58.0	60.5
1939	61.0	60.0	60.5	61.5	61.0	61.5	58.5	59.5	68.5	73.5	76.5	79.0

TABLE 2.10 : SAUERBECK-STATIST WHOLESALE PRICE INDEX : FOOD.
SEASONALLY ADJUSTED (1924 AVERAGE = 100)

	JAN	FEB	MAR	APR	MAY	JUN	JUL	AUG	SEP	OCT	NOV	DEC
1919	140	140	131	128	131	135	[illegible]	141	144	151	154	158
1920	159	170	176	181	184	191	191	185	182	181	174	154
1921	150	139	136	129	122	122	121	120	113	101	100	97
1922	97	99	102	105	104	105	102	96	94	96	97	99
1923	96	97	96	95	94	90	91	90	94	93	94	96
1924	99	98	94	94	96	97	97	98	103	108	105	110
1925	109	106	102	98	99	94	95	97	94	93	94	96
1926	92	90	88	90	90	93	93	94	93	92	92	91
1927	90	88	88	89	90	90	87	89	87	85	87	86
1928	86	88	92	92	95	92	88	86	85	86	87	85
1929	85	86	85	84	81	83	86	85	84	84	82	81
1930	81	78	75	75	72	72	72	70	71	72	69	68
1931	68	65	66	65	64	65	63	63	64	64	64	66
1932	65	66	65	64	64	59	61	60	60	58	57	57
1933	57	57	57	58	57	57	58	58	57	57	57	57
1934	59	60	58	58	59	59	62	63	60	60	60	60
1935	59	59	58	59	60	59	58	59	59	60	60	59
1936	60	60	59	59	60	60	61	63	64	66	67	67
1937	67	69	73	72	73	73	72	72	72	73	72	71
1938	70	70	69	69	68	68	64	62	61	60	59	60
1939	61	60	60	61	61	62	58	59	68	74	78	79

TABLE 2.11 : SAUERBECK-STATIST WHOLESALE PRICE INDEX : RAW MATERIALS (1924 AVERAGE = 100)

	JAN	FEB	MAR	APR	MAY	JUN	JUL	AUG	SEP	OCT	NOV	DEC
1919	134.9	131.2	131.9	131.9	142.4	147.9	147.9	157.9	159.1	167.1	173.3	177.7
1920	186.9	196.8	193.1	192.5	184.5	176.4	175.2	176.4	175.2	166.5	151.7	146.7
1921	135.6	126.3	120.7	113.9	110.2	104.0	107.7	102.1	104.0	98.4	96.6	96.0
1922	94.1	92.2	90.4	88.5	91.0	91.6	91.0	89.8	89.8	91.6	91.6	89.8
1923	91.6	92.9	93.5	94.7	93.5	91.6	87.9	87.9	89.8	91.0	96.0	96.6
1924	97.8	100.3	100.3	98.4	97.8	96.6	99.7	97.8	99.7	102.8	104.0	104.6
1925	101.5	100.9	98.4	97.2	94.7	93.5	96.0	94.7	95.3	94.1	96.6	93.5
1926	92.9	91.6	91.0	88.5	88.5	87.9	88.5	89.8	91.0	96.0	96.0	87.3
1927	87.3	88.5	87.9	86.7	86.7	86.7	87.6	87.9	87.6	88.5	88.5	87.3
1928	86.7	85.4	85.4	87.3	86.0	84.8	84.8	84.2	83.6	83.6	84.2	83.6
1929	84.0	86.0	87.0	82.0	80.5	79.5	80.5	80.0	79.5	78.0	76.0	76.0
1930	74.0	73.0	72.0	70.0	69.0	66.5	65.0	64.0	62.5	61.5	61.0	59.0
1931	58.0	59.0	58.5	57.0	55.0	56.0	54.0	53.0	55.0	56.5	57.5	58.5
1932	58.5	59.5	57.0	54.0	52.5	52.5	54.0	57.0	56.5	55.5	55.5	55.0
1933	55.0	54.5	54.0	55.5	58.5	59.5	59.5	58.5	58.0	58.5	57.5	57.5
1934	59.0	59.0	59.5	58.5	58.0	57.0	57.0	58.0	58.0	57.5	58.0	59.0
1935	60.0	60.0	60.0	61.0	62.0	61.0	61.5	61.5	62.0	63.0	64.0	64.0
1936	63.5	64.0	64.0	63.0	62.0	61.0	63.0	64.5	65.0	66.0	69.0	73.0
1937	73.5	76.0	79.5	76.0	77.5	77.0	77.5	76.0	75.0	72.0	69.0	69.0
1938	68.5	69.0	66.5	66.0	64.0	64.5	65.5	64.5	65.5	66.5	66.0	66.5
1939	66.5	66.0	66.0	67.5	68.0	67.5	67.0	68.5	73.5	77.5	83.5	91.0

TABLE 2.12 : SAUERBECK-STATIST WHOLESALE PRICE INDEX : RAW MATERIALS. SEASONALLY ADJUSTED (1924 AVERAGE = 100)

	JAN	FEB	MAR	APR	MAY	JUN	JUL	AUG	SEP	OCT	NOV	DEC
1919	134	129	131	132	144	152	150	160	159	166	171	175
1920	185	194	192	193	187	181	178	179	175	165	149	145
1921	134	124	120	114	111	107	109	104	104	98	95	95
1922	93	91	90	89	92	94	92	91	90	91	90	89
1923	91	91	93	95	95	94	89	89	90	90	95	95
1924	97	99	100	99	99	99	101	99	99	102	102	103
1925	100	99	98	98	96	96	97	96	95	93	95	92
1926	93	90	90	89	90	90	90	90	91	95	94	87
1927	87	87	87	88	88	88	89	88	87	87	87	87
1928	86	84	84	88	88	86	86	85	83	82	83	83
1929	84	85	86	83	82	81	82	80	79	77	75	76
1930	74	72	71	71	70	68	66	64	62	61	60	59
1931	58	58	58	58	56	57	55	53	55	56	57	58
1932	58	59	56	55	53	54	55	57	56	55	55	55
1933	55	54	54	56	58	60	59	59	58	59	58	57
1934	59	59	59	59	58	58	57	58	58	58	58	59
1935	60	60	60	61	62	62	61	62	62	63	64	64
1936	63	63	64	63	62	62	63	65	65	66	69	73
1937	73	75	79	76	77	78	77	76	75	72	69	69
1938	68	68	66	66	64	65	65	65	66	67	66	66
1939	66	65	66	68	68	68	67	69	74	78	84	91

TABLE 2.13 : MINISTRY OF LABOUR RETAIL PRICE INDEX : COST OF LIVING.
(1924 AVERAGE = 100)

	JAN	FEB	MAR	APR	MAY	JUN	JUL	AUG	SEP	OCT	NOV	DEC
1919	125.6	122.8	119.9	117.1	117.1	118.2	122.8	122.8	125.6	128.5	128.5	128.5
1920	131.3	131.3	132.5	137.6	142.8	143.9	145.6	149.0	150.7	157.6	153.6	151.3
1921	143.3	137.6	133.0	130.2	125.1	125.1	126.8	125.6	119.9	115.9	113.6	109.6
1922	107.4	106.2	103.9	103.4	102.8	105.1	103.4	102.2	101.6	102.8	102.8	101.6
1923	101.1	100.5	99.4	97.1	96.5	96.5	97.6	98.8	99.9	99.9	101.1	101.1
1924	102.2	101.6	98.8	97.6	96.5	97.1	97.6	98.2	100.5	102.8	103.4	102.8
1925	102.2	102.2	99.9	98.8	98.2	98.8	98.8	99.4	100.5	100.5	101.1	99.9
1926	98.8	98.2	95.9	95.4	95.9	97.1	97.1	98.2	99.4	102.2	102.2	99.9
1927	98.2	97.6	94.2	93.6	93.1	94.8	94.2	94.2	95.4	96.5	96.5	95.9
1928	94.8	93.6	93.6	93.6	94.2	94.2	94.2	94.2	94.8	95.4	95.9	95.4
1929	94.0	95.0	92.5	92.0	91.5	92.0	93.0	93.5	94.5	95.5	95.5	95.0
1930	94.0	92.0	90.0	89.0	88.0	88.5	89.5	89.5	89.0	89.5	88.5	87.5
1931	87.0	86.0	84.0	84.0	83.0	84.0	83.0	83.0	83.0	83.5	84.5	84.0
1932	84.0	83.5	82.5	81.5	81.0	81.5	80.5	80.5	81.5	81.5	81.5	81.0
1933	80.5	79.5	78.5	77.5	77.5	79.0	79.5	80.5	80.5	80.5	81.5	81.0
1934	80.5	80.0	79.5	78.5	79.0	80.5	81.0	81.5	81.5	82.5	82.5	81.5
1935	81.0	80.5	79.5	79.5	80.0	81.5	81.5	81.5	83.0	84.0	84.0	84.0
1936	84.0	83.5	82.5	82.5	82.5	83.5	83.5	84.0	84.5	86.5	86.5	86.5
1937	86.5	86.5	86.5	87.0	87.0	88.5	88.5	88.5	90.0	91.5	91.5	91.0
1938	89.5	89.0	88.0	89.0	88.5	91.0	89.0	89.0	88.5	89.0	89.0	88.5
1939	88.5	87.5	87.5	87.5	87.5	89.0	88.5	88.5	94.5	96.5	99.0	99.5

TABLE 2.14 : MINISTRY OF LABOUR RETAIL PRICE INDEX : COST OF LIVING.
SEASONALLY ADJUSTED (1924 AVERAGE = 100)

	JAN	FEB	MAR	APR	MAY	JUN	JUL	AUG	SEP	OCT	NOV	DEC
1919	125	123	122	120	120	120	123	122	124	125	125	127
1920	131	132	135	140	146	146	146	149	149	154	150	149
1921	143	138	135	133	128	127	127	125	119	113	111	108
1922	107	106	106	106	105	106	104	102	101	100	100	100
1923	101	101	101	99	99	98	98	99	99	97	99	100
1924	102	102	101	100	99	98	98	98	99	100	101	101
1925	102	102	102	101	100	100	99	99	99	98	99	99
1926	98	98	97	97	98	98	98	98	99	100	100	98
1927	97	97	96	95	95	96	95	94	95	95	94	94
1928	94	93	95	95	96	95	95	94	94	94	94	94
1929	93	95	94	94	93	93	94	94	94	94	93	94
1930	93	92	91	91	90	89	90	90	88	88	87	86
1931	86	86	85	86	85	85	84	83	82	82	83	83
1932	83	83	84	83	83	82	81	81	81	80	80	80
1933	80	80	80	79	79	79	80	80	80	79	80	80
1934	80	80	81	80	81	81	81	81	81	81	81	81
1935	81	81	81	81	82	82	82	81	82	83	83	83
1936	84	84	84	84	84	84	84	84	84	85	85	86
1937	86	87	88	89	89	89	89	88	89	90	90	90
1938	89	89	89	91	90	91	89	89	88	88	87	88
1939	88	88	89	89	89	89	89	88	94	95	97	98

TABLE 2.15 : MINISTRY OF LABOUR RETAIL PRICE INDEX : FOOD
(1924 AVERAGE = 100)

	JAN	FEB	MAR	APR	MAY	JUN	JUL	AUG	SEP	OCT	NOV	DEC
1919	135.0	129.1	125.0	121.5	119.8	122.7	127.4	126.8	130.3	135.6	137.4	138.5
1920	138.0	136.8	138.0	144.4	149.7	151.5	153.8	156.7	158.5	170.8	165.5	163.2
1921	154.4	146.2	139.7	136.2	128.0	129.1	132.7	132.1	123.3	117.4	114.5	108.6
1922	105.1	103.9	101.6	101.0	99.8	105.7	102.7	101.0	101.0	103.3	104.5	102.7
1923	101.6	100.4	98.6	95.1	93.9	95.1	96.9	98.6	101.0	101.6	103.3	102.7
1924	103.9	103.3	98.0	95.7	93.9	95.1	96.3	97.4	101.0	105.1	105.7	104.5
1925	103.3	103.3	99.8	98.0	97.4	98.0	98.6	99.8	101.0	101.0	102.1	100.4
1926	98.6	96.9	93.3	92.8	92.8	94.5	94.5	95.1	95.7	99.2	99.2	98.0
1927	96.3	95.1	91.0	90.4	90.4	93.3	91.6	92.2	94.5	95.7	95.7	95.1
1928	93.3	91.0	91.0	90.4	91.6	92.2	91.6	91.6	92.2	93.3	93.9	93.3
1929	91.5	92.0	88.0	87.5	86.0	87.5	90.0	90.5	91.5	93.5	93.5	92.0
1930	90.5	88.0	84.0	82.0	81.0	83.0	84.5	84.5	84.0	84.5	83.0	81.0
1931	80.0	79.0	76.0	76.0	75.0	76.0	75.0	75.0	75.0	76.5	77.5	77.0
1932	77.0	76.0	74.0	73.0	72.0	73.5	72.0	72.0	73.5	73.5	73.5	72.0
1933	71.5	70.0	67.5	67.0	67.0	69.5	70.0	71.5	72.0	74.0	74.0	73.0
1934	71.5	70.5	69.5	68.0	68.5	71.5	72.0	74.0	73.5	74.5	74.5	73.5
1935	73.0	71.5	70.0	69.5	70.5	74.0	74.0	73.5	75.0	77.0	77.0	77.0
1936	76.5	75.5	74.0	73.5	74.0	75.5	75.5	77.0	77.5	80.0	80.0	80.0
1937	79.5	79.5	79.5	80.0	80.0	82.0	82.0	82.0	84.0	85.5	85.5	85.0
1938	83.5	82.0	80.5	81.5	81.0	85.5	83.0	82.0	81.5	82.0	81.5	81.0
1939	81.0	79.0	79.0	78.5	78.5	81.5	80.5	81.0	88.0	90.5	92.0	92.0

TABLE 2.16 : MINISTRY OF LABOUR RETAIL PRICE INDEX : FOOD.
SEASONALLY ADJUSTED (1924 AVERAGE = 100)

	JAN	FEB	MAR	APR	MAY	JUN	JUL	AUG	SEP	OCT	NOV	DEC
1919	134	129	128	126	125	125	128	127	129	130	132	135
1920	137	137	142	149	156	154	155	156	157	164	159	159
1921	153	147	143	141	133	132	134	132	122	113	110	106
1922	104	104	104	104	104	108	104	101	100	99	100	100
1923	101	101	101	98	98	97	98	98	100	98	99	100
1924	103	104	101	99	98	97	97	97	100	101	101	102
1925	102	104	102	101	102	100	99	100	100	97	98	98
1926	97	97	96	96	96	96	95	95	95	96	96	96
1927	95	95	93	93	94	94	92	92	94	93	93	93
1928	92	91	93	93	95	93	92	92	91	91	91	91
1929	90	92	90	90	89	88	91	91	91	91	90	90
1930	89	88	86	85	84	84	85	85	83	82	80	79
1931	79	79	78	78	78	77	76	75	74	74	75	75
1932	76	76	76	75	74	74	73	72	73	71	71	70
1933	71	71	70	70	70	69	70	71	71	72	72	72
1934	71	71	72	71	71	71	72	73	73	72	72	72
1935	72	72	72	72	73	74	74	73	74	75	75	75
1936	76	76	76	76	77	75	75	76	76	77	78	78
1937	79	80	82	83	83	82	82	81	83	83	83	83
1938	83	83	83	85	84	85	83	81	80	79	79	79
1939	80	80	81	82	82	81	80	80	87	88	89	90

TABLE 2.17 : INDEX OF RETAIL SALES : FOOD AND PERISHABLES
(1937 AVERAGE = 100)

	JAN	FEB	MAR	APR	MAY	JUN	JUL	AUG	SEP	OCT	NOV	DEC
1932	77	78	77	84	76	82	74	73	75	76	77	88
1933	73	75	75	80	74	79	72	72	74	76	78	90
1934	75	77	79	80	79	80	75	75	77	78	80	92
1935	78	81	81	86	84	86	81	80	83	86	88	101
1936	88	88	89	94	89	93	88	87	89	92	94	109
1937	91	94	104	95	107	97	97	94	97	100	102	120
1938	99	102	102	110	103	107	102	99	102	103	102	122
1939	98	103	105	113	112	105	106	103	114	113	108	125

TABLE 2.18 : INDEX OF RETAIL SALES : FOOD AND PERISHABLES
SEASONALLY ADJUSTED (1937 AVERAGE = 100)

	JAN	FEB	MAR	APR	MAY	JUN	JUL	AUG	SEP	OCT	NOV	DEC
1932	80	79	77	81	75	81	77	77	78	77	77	76
1933	76	76	75	77	73	78	75	76	77	77	78	78
1934	78	78	79	77	78	79	78	80	80	79	80	80
1935	81	82	81	83	83	85	84	85	86	87	88	87
1936	92	89	89	91	88	92	92	92	92	93	94	94
1937	95	95	104	92	106	96	101	100	100	101	102	104
1938	103	104	102	106	102	106	106	105	105	104	102	106
1939	102	105	105	109	111	104	110	109	118	115	108	108

TABLE 2.19 : INDEX OF RETAIL SALES : OTHER MERCHANDISE
(1937 AVERAGE = 100)

	JAN	FEB	MAR	APR	MAY	JUN	JUL	AUG	SEP	OCT	NOV	DEC
1932	85	65	74	84	85	90	89	63	77	86	83	117
1933	78	63	72	88	88	86	90	64	75	87	86	124
1934	82	65	77	84	95	89	92	68	78	91	90	126
1935	85	67	75	94	94	93	98	69	84	95	94	136
1936	93	71	79	94	102	94	100	73	85	103	100	142
1937	94	77	90	97	109	98	106	76	92	102	105	152
1938	98	76	84	103	100	105	109	77	89	103	102	154
1939	98	79	86	103	109	100	107	83	103	106	98	146

TABLE 2.20 : INDEX OF RETAIL SALES : OTHER MERCHANDISE
SEASONALLY ADJUSTED (1937 AVERAGE = 100)

	JAN	FEB	MAR	APR	MAY	JUN	JUL	AUG	SEP	OCT	NOV	DEC
1932	86	83	84	81	78	87	82	81	84	81	80	78
1933	79	81	82	85	81	83	83	82	82	82	83	83
1934	83	83	88	81	88	86	84	87	85	86	86	84
1935	86	86	85	91	87	90	90	89	91	90	90	91
1936	94	91	90	91	94	91	92	94	92	98	96	95
1937	95	99	102	94	101	95	97	98	100	97	101	102
1938	99	97	96	100	92	102	100	99	97	98	98	103
1939	99	101	98	100	101	97	98	107	112	100	94	98

TABLE 2.21 : INDEX OF RETAIL SALES : TOTAL
(1937 AVERAGE = 100)

	JAN	FEB	MAR	APR	MAY	JUN	JUL	AUG	SEP	OCT	NOV	DEC
1932	80	71	75	84	81	86	82	68	75	81	80	102
1933	75	69	73	84	81	82	81	68	74	81	82	106
1934	78	71	78	82	87	84	83	71	77	84	85	108
1935	81	74	78	90	89	89	89	75	83	90	91	118
1936	90	80	84	94	95	93	94	80	87	97	97	125
1937	93	86	97	96	108	98	102	85	95	101	104	135
1938	98	89	93	107	101	106	105	88	96	103	102	138
1939	98	91	96	108	111	103	107	94	109	109	103	136

TABLE 2.22 : INDEX OF RETAIL SALES : TOTAL
SEASONALLY ADJUSTED (1937 AVERAGE = 100)

	JAN	FEB	MAR	APR	MAY	JUN	JUL	AUG	SEP	OCT	NOV	DEC
1932	83	80	80	81	77	84	80	79	80	80	78	77
1933	77	78	78	81	77	81	79	79	79	80	80	80
1934	80	80	83	79	83	82	81	83	82	83	83	82
1935	84	84	83	87	85	87	87	87	88	88	89	90
1936	93	91	89	91	91	91	92	93	93	95	95	95
1937	96	97	103	93	103	96	100	99	101	99	102	102
1938	101	101	99	104	97	104	103	102	102	101	100	105
1939	101	103	102	105	106	101	104	109	116	107	101	103

3 Level of Business Activity

TABLES

SOURCES

Tables 3.1–3.9 *The Economist*

Table 3.10 E. H. Phelps-Brown and G. L. S. Shackle, 'An index of real turnover, 1919–36', *Oxford Economic Papers*, I (1938), pp. 32–48.

All the tables in the first part of this section (3.1–3.9) are derived from *The Economist*'s index of business activity. Table 3.1 presents the combined index, whilst the other tables provide some of the major components of that index that do not appear elsewhere in this collection. The combined index was published regularly in *The Economist* 'Trade supplement' from October 1933 but was extended back to 1920 by *The Economist* by using component series which had been appearing frequently in the publication for a long time.

The figures appearing before 1936 were converted by *The*

Economist to a 1924 base, and later figures to a 1935 base.[1] For consistency in our tables all the later data have been converted to a 1924 base by means of a simple arithmetic transformation made possible by the original 1935 data being available on the 1924 base. The main index and all but one of the component series were seasonally adjusted at source, the seasonal coefficient being calculated 'on a "moving" basis consisting of a series of years up to and including the year previous to that for which the indices are calculated'.[2] The only exception was the index of merchandise on railways where seasonal adjustment was considered impossible because the data related to four weekly periods ending at different times of the month. 'In the case of indices which refer to industries that are either contracting or expanding more rapidly than the average of all industries, this long-period trend has been eliminated before computing seasonal variations.'[3]

The combined index consisted of fourteen component indices[4] (weightings are given in parentheses immediatedly after the title of each component):

1 *Total employment* (10) – as published in the Ministry of Labour's *Gazette* for insured workers – see Chapter 4 for more details on this series.

2 *Consumption of coal* (4) – the output of saleable coal by the domestic industry, minus both exports (including foreign bunker coal) and the consumption of coal in steel production. The data are daily averages.

3 *Industrial consumption of electricity* (2) – 'Based on output of authorised undertakers, less units generated for domestic purposes and for use in traction and public lighting. Adjusted for transfer from private to public generation.' Daily averages were used.

4 *Merchandise on railways* (4) – based on the tonnage of freight carried, less coal and coke. Daily averages used.

5 *Commercial motor vehicles in use* (2) – for the period until June 1936 this was based on the official quarterly return of the number of commercial licences currently in use. For July 1936

onwards the series used was 'the number of goods vehicles in use' as compiled by the Society for Motor Manufacturers and Traders. Daily averages used.

6 *Postal receipts* (3) – were daily averages of Post Office data.

7 *Building activity* (2) – *The Economist*'s definition was that: This index is based on a twelve-month moving average of the figures showing the value of building plans passed by 146 local authorities in England and Wales . . . A twelve-month moving average has been chosen on the assumption that twelve months elapse, on the average, between the passing of the plans and the completion of the buildings. The index is corrected by a specially constructed index of building costs explained in *The Economist* of November 11, 1933.'

8 *Consumption of iron and steel* (2) – measured the output of steel ingots and castings, forge and foundry pig-iron, plus the 'crude steel equivalent' of net imports. Daily averages used.

9 *Consumption of cotton* (1) – based on the daily average of deliveries (lb) to spinners.

10 *Imports of raw materials* (2) – daily averages of the value of imports, less re-exports, deflated by the appropriate Board of Trade price index.

11 *Exports of manufactures* (3) – daily averages of the value of exports, corrected by use of the Board of Trade prices.

12 *Shipping movements* (2) – measured shipping tonnage entered and cleared in overseas trade. Daily averages used.

13 *Metropolitan, Country and Provincial bank clearings* (4) – 'Based on monthly clearing figures, corrected by an index of prices composed of the Ministry of Labour index of wages (two weights), the Ministry of Labour index of the cost of living (two weights), and *The Economist*'s index of wholesale prices (one weight).' Converted to daily averages.

14 *Town bank clearings* (1) – using the series for Town clearings, corrected as for 13.

The combined index is a geometric mean, weighted as shown. The usefulness and accuracy of the index were considered by the compilers to be much less for the years before 1924. The *Economist* saw the index as 'an attempt to measure changes in the economic activity of the country quantitatively and not in terms of values; in other words, it is intended to give an approximate indication of variations in "real" national income'. Thus, all value series were adjusted for price movements, but most of the data were volume series. In total the series gives a much broader coverage than the quarterly indices of industrial production which were available to contemporaries.

The other main index of aggregate economic activity presented here is the Phelps-Brown and Shackle 'Index of real turnover', shown in Table 3.10. For construction of the index the total of Metropolitan, Country and Provincial bank clearings was regarded as 'an index of the flow of cheque-payments in the non-financial circulation of the United Kingdom' and this, in turn, was adjusted by use of 'a specially constructed index-number of the prices of the goods and services for which these cheque-payments were made'. The resulting index was considered to be a measure of real turnover, or of 'the physical amount of goods and services traded'.[5]

The main series adjusted by Phelps-Brown and Shackle was the sum of the two London bank clearings, 'Metropolitan' and 'Country', plus the Provincial clearings. As the aim was to derive an index of non-financial payments the 'Town' clearing was excluded as this was dominated by the financial dealings of the City of London, especially those arising out of Stock Exchange transactions. The two London series used were published by the committee of London clearing banks and largely applied to the business of members of that committee, although they also included the business of banks for which committee members acted as agents; plus a limited amount of Bank of England business. The 'Metropolitan' clearing covered the payment of cheques, bills and other drafts at offices within half-an-hour's journey of the centre of the City, excluding 'Town' clearings. The 'Country' clearing applied to all cheques drawn on branches of Clearing House members outside the 'Town' and 'Metropolitan' clearings, plus those drawn on provincial banks with agency arrangements.

Business here was restricted to England and Wales. The non-London Provincial clearings dealt with the bulk of provincial business not covered by the 'Country' clearing. These were local clearings based at major provincial centres.[6]

The bank clearing series was adjusted by Phelps-Brown and Shackle to take account of the presence of seasonal variations, and a 'non-deflatable' element was deducted. It was then converted to a 'real' index by dividing through by a specially-constructed composite price index. The weighting of components within the price index is based on the relative importance of different types of payments within the total 'cheque-paid, non-financial circulation' of 1930.[7] The types of payment correspond to transactions covered by the following price/cost series (weights are given in parentheses):

1 Board of Trade index of wholesale prices, all articles (93). Old index 1919–29, new index 1930–6.

2 Board of Trade index of wholesale prices, industrial items (378). Old index 1919–29, new index 1930–6. For 1919 only no. 1 was used.

3 Ministry of Labour cost-of-living index, all items (355).

4 Ministry of Labour cost-of-living index, rent (29).

5 London and Cambridge Economic Service, weekly wage index (70).

6 Board of Trade quarterly index of the average value of exports of U.K. goods (75) – from 1924 only. Interpolation was used to calculate monthly figures, and for 1919–23 this series was substituted by no. 1.

NOTES

1 'Trade Supplement' 158, 25 July 1936, pp. 2–5 in *The Economist*, CXXIV.

2 'Trade Supplement' 145, 29 June 1935, p. 43, in *The Economist*, CXX.

3 *Ibid.*

4 The original series appearing in 1933 consisted of eighteen variables but the series shown here is in the form revised in 1935. Definitions are from the 'Trade Supplement' 145, 29 June 1935, p. 47, in *The Economist*, CXX.

5 Both quotes from E. H. Phelps-Brown and G. L. S. Shackle, 'An index of real turnover, 1919–36' *Oxford Economic Papers*, I (1938), p. 32.

6 See Chapter 7 for further details.

7 Phelps-Brown and Shackle, p. 45.

TABLE 3.1 : THE ECONOMIST INDEX OF BUSINESS ACTIVITY
SEASONALLY ADJUSTED (1924 AVERAGE = 100)

	JAN	FEB	MAR	APR	MAY	JUN	JUL	AUG	SEP	OCT	NOV	DEC
1920	98.5	104.0	99.5	102.5	106.5	103.0	103.0	106.5	103.0	92.0	92.0	91.0
1921	90.5	84.5	76.5	30.5	33.5	38.0	69.0	80.0	82.0	82.5	81.5	78.0
1922	76.5	80.5	80.5	82.5	83.0	84.0	88.0	91.5	89.5	91.5	90.5	91.0
1923	93.0	93.5	94.0	92.5	93.5	95.5	90.0	92.5	96.5	96.5	95.0	98.5
1924	93.5	98.5	98.0	99.0	101.5	100.5	101.0	100.5	101.0	101.5	101.5	100.5
1925	101.5	101.0	101.5	101.0	99.0	100.0	100.5	98.5	100.5	100.5	103.0	104.5
1926	104.0	105.5	104.5	106.0	44.5	53.5	54.5	73.0	79.5	85.5	90.5	102.0
1927	108.5	108.5	111.5	109.0	110.5	109.0	107.5	107.5	109.5	108.5	107.0	104.5
1928	105.5	106.5	107.0	108.0	107.0	106.5	106.0	107.0	108.0	108.0	107.5	109.0
1929	110.0	108.5	110.0	111.5	111.0	112.0	111.5	113.5	113.0	113.5	113.5	111.5
1930	110.5	111.0	109.5	107.5	107.0	106.5	104.5	103.5	103.5	103.5	102.5	100.0
1931	97.5	98.0	98.5	98.5	99.0	98.0	98.5	98.0	96.5	97.5	100.0	99.5
1932	96.5	98.0	99.0	95.5	95.5	96.5	94.5	93.0	93.5	96.0	94.5	96.0
1933	95.5	97.5	97.0	98.0	98.5	99.5	100.5	103.0	105.5	104.5	106.5	107.0
1934	110.0	108.5	109.0	108.0	107.0	108.5	107.5	110.0	110.5	111.0	110.5	110.5
1935	110.5	111.0	109.5	112.5	113.5	114.0	112.5	113.0	115.5	116.5	117.0	119.0
1936	116.0	116.5	116.5	119.4	118.8	120.5	121.7	123.4	123.4	122.8	122.8	124.5
1937	122.2	124.5	126.2	124.5	127.9	128.5	126.8	129.0	129.0	128.5	127.9	126.2
1938	126.8	125.1	121.7	118.8	116.0	117.1	116.0	116.0	118.2	118.2	116.0	114.8

TABLE 3.2 : INDEX OF COAL CONSUMPTION
SEASONALLY ADJUSTED (1924 AVERAGE =100)

	JAN	FEB	MAR	APR	MAY	JUN	JUL	AUG	SEP	OCT	NOV	DEC
1920	93.5	107.0	94.0	108.0	114.5	117.5	114.0	124.5	113.0	98.5	89.0	75.5
1921	98.5	88.5	83.5	0.0	6.0	8.0	96.0	97.5	89.0	86.0	89.5	83.0
1922	83.5	89.5	84.5	90.0	91.5	82.5	95.0	104.0	88.0	98.5	94.0	88.0
1923	97.5	92.5	93.0	92.0	96.0	107.5	93.5	96.5	99.0	99.0	98.5	93.5
1924	92.5	105.0	103.0	105.0	104.0	99.0	100.0	101.0	102.0	100.0	100.0	92.5
1925	95.0	79.5	95.5	94.0	93.5	94.5	110.0	89.0	90.0	84.5	95.5	98.0
1926	98.0	98.5	98.0	111.5	0.0	0.0	0.0	9.5	16.5	35.0	55.5	106.5
1927	95.5	97.0	92.0	97.0	102.5	104.5	103.5	99.0	103.0	97.5	95.0	95.0
1928	95.5	91.0	92.0	92.0	92.0	93.5	91.5	93.5	94.5	92.5	91.5	92.0
1929	98.5	100.0	97.5	89.5	94.5	99.5	96.0	105.0	98.5	96.5	97.5	95.0
1930	96.5	98.5	92.0	92.5	93.0	89.0	89.0	95.0	88.0	91.0	96.5	91.5
1931	84.5	88.0	86.0	87.0	85.5	89.5	85.5	85.0	86.0	87.0	86.0	89.5
1932	83.0	87.5	89.0	82.0	85.5	83.5	78.5	80.5	83.0	87.0	86.0	89.5
1933	88.5	86.0	80.5	80.0	83.0	80.5	79.5	84.5	88.5	87.0	90.5	91.5
1934	103.5	89.5	94.0	89.0	88.5	85.5	85.0	93.0	91.0	93.0	96.0	90.0
1935	93.0	93.0	87.0	92.5	97.0	94.5	88.0	89.5	86.5	101.0	100.5	102.[illegible]
1936	102.2	96.0	93.7	98.4	97.9	95.1	89.8	99.4	97.9	99.4	99.4	102.[illegible]
1937	93.1	103.7	105.1	107.0	110.3	109.9	101.8	102.2	105.6	100.8	102.7	100.[illegible]
1938	103.2	103.7	97.9	94.6	99.8	100.3	97.0	93.6	100.3	99.4	93.1	96.[illegible]
1939	100.3	98.9	100.3	107.5								

TABLE 3.3 : INDEX OF IRON AND STEEL CONSUMPTION
SEASONALLY ADJUSTED (1924 AXERAGE = 100)

	JAN	FEB	MAR	APR	MAY	JUN	JUL	AUG	SEP	OCT	NOV	DEC
1920	103.0	106.0	91.0	102.0	101.0	114.0	97.5	119.0	122.0	73.0	63.5	141.0
1921	90.0	85.0	64.0	3.5	0.0	3.5	26.5	83.5	75.0	68.5	66.5	58.5
1922	32.5	41.0	43.0	38.0	38.0	39.0	53.5	70.0	64.5	63.0	58.0	78.0
1923	78.0	85.0	84.5	81.5	77.5	88.0	84.5	82.5	89.0	76.0	77.5	95.0
1924	91.0	97.0	105.0	94.5	108.0	91.0	108.0	92.0	101.0	103.0	104.0	99.0
1925	97.5	98.0	94.0	96.5	86.5	89.0	85.5	91.0	94.5	83.5	93.0	99.5
1926	95.5	94.5	89.0	101.0	0.0	6.0	7.5	32.5	55.0	43.0	51.5	108.0
1927	174.0	163.0	151.0	153.0	125.0	120.0	113.0	115.0	114.0	112.5	98.5	111.0
1928	104.0	111.0	95.0	95.5	93.0	92.5	96.0	105.0	103.0	100.0	94.5	105.0
1929	98.5	108.0	103.0	111.0	95.5	129.0	109.0	127.0	129.0	118.0	128.0	119.0
1930	122.0	118.0	113.0	92.0	95.5	98.5	96.0	88.0	98.5	83.0	78.0	86.5
1931	77.5	84.5	82.0	67.5	83.5	83.5	80.0	82.0	79.5	91.5	106.0	96.0
1932	78.5	93.0	68.0	63.0	65.5	69.5	67.5	59.5	65.5	72.0	56.5	66.5
1933	64.0	72.5	70.5	75.0	71.5	77.5	80.0	86.5	93.0	88.5	93.0	114.5
1934	117.5	106.5	112.5	106.5	104.0	103.0	107.0	107.0	106.0	109.5	103.0	117.0
1935	117.0	110.5	115.0	105.5	106.0	113.0	109.0	122.5	123.5	120.0	118.5	138.0
1936	136.4	134.0	131.1	146.8	135.2	141.0	143.3	162.0	153.8	148.6	145.7	156.7
1937	144.5	137.5	138.1	136.4	152.1	155.6	163.2	186.5	183.6	184.7	194.6	202.2
1938	197.5	180.6	166.7	143.5	121.8	108.4	106.1	104.9	104.3	118.9	115.4	95.6
1939	117.1	136.9	151.5	170.1	177.1	183.6	186.5					

TABLE 3.4 : INDEX OF COTTON CONSUMPTION
SEASONALLY ADJUSTED (1924 AVERAGE = 100)

	JAN	FEB	MAR	APR	MAY	JUN	JUL	AUG	SEP	OCT	NOV	DEC
1920	165.0	183.0	154.0	131.0	115.5	110.5	114.0	126.0	97.0	79.5	86.0	83.0
1921	78.5	66.5	51.0	54.0	43.5	29.5	84.5	101.0	111.5	104.0	89.0	78.0
1922	81.0	80.5	85.5	88.5	107.0	117.0	132.0	117.0	109.0	93.0	86.5	87.5
1923	91.0	103.5	84.0	80.0	78.5	73.5	78.5	85.5	88.0	96.0	83.0	101.0
1924	97.0	98.0	92.5	95.5	102.0	88.0	88.0	93.0	100.0	107.5	115.0	114.5
1925	128.0	122.0	119.0	118.5	114.5	118.5	115.0	111.5	111.5	118.0	118.0	122.0
1926	123.0	114.0	111.0	110.5	64.5	98.0	86.0	96.0	101.0	100.0	94.5	109.0
1927	118.5	122.5	134.0	114.0	118.0	98.0	123.0	124.5	117.5	102.0	97.0	92.5
1928	78.0	112.0	109.5	109.0	102.0	117.0	111.5	98.5	127.5	105.0	103.0	109.0
1929	108.5	102.5	107.5	107.0	106.0	122.0	99.0	83.5	101.5	108.0	101.5	101.5
1930	100.5	88.5	87.0	84.0	83.5	68.5	59.5	76.5	64.5	74.0	74.5	63.5
1931	61.0	64.0	75.5	71.5	71.5	79.0	80.5	97.5	81.0	89.0	97.5	97.0
1932	92.5	89.5	94.5	97.5	91.0	92.0	93.0	83.0	72.0	86.0	75.0	88.5
1933	88.0	90.0	84.5	85.5	90.0	98.0	108.0	110.5	103.0	92.0	97.0	90.5
1934	95.5	98.5	87.5	93.5	93.5	103.0	97.0	95.5	91.0	85.0	81.0	87.0
1935	90.0	86.0	89.5	85.5	90.5	97.5	108.0	97.0	90.0	91.5	101.0	93.0
1936	99.4	93.3	94.7	102.6	105.0	111.0	111.9	111.9	99.8	95.6	93.8	101.7
1937	104.1	102.6	114.7	108.7	133.4	103.6	105.9	107.7	98.9	100.3	99.4	90.5
1938	99.8	94.7	95.2	77.0	75.6	75.6	78.8	88.6	81.6	75.6	75.6	76.5
1939	77.9	82.6	87.7	104.6	105.9	103.1	103.6	101.7				

TABLE 3.5 : INDEX OF MERCHANDISE CARRIED ON RAILWAYS (1924 AVERAGE = 100)

	JAN	FEB	MAR	APR	MAY	JUN	JUL	AUG	SEP	OCT	NOV	DEC
1920	102.0	109.0	111.0	111.0	111.0	108.0	105.0	106.5	109.5	99.0	96.5	98.5
1921	88.5	87.0	84.5	65.0	51.5	48.5	55.0	70.5	75.0	75.5	75.0	70.5
1922	67.0	76.0	81.5	80.0	80.5	77.5	76.5	80.5	83.5	89.0	89.0	90.0
1923	89.0	92.5	101.0	103.0	101.5	97.5	89.5	92.0	94.5	98.5	98.0	96.0
1924	84.5	100.0	105.5	107.5	103.5	101.5	97.5	97.5	100.5	104.0	101.5	96.5
1925	96.0	99.5	101.5	102.0	98.5	95.5	93.5	91.0	99.0	98.0	99.0	94.5
1926	91.5	102.0	105.0	106.0	46.5	74.5	65.5	70.0	74.5	76.0	76.5	84.0
1927	91.5	99.0	106.5	107.5	108.0	102.0	96.0	96.5	96.5	100.0	101.0	93.5
1928	84.5	93.5	95.0	98.0	96.0	92.0	89.0	90.0	92.5	95.0	94.5	92.0
1929	86.5	84.0	95.5	103.0	99.5	96.5	94.5	95.5	98.5	101.5	98.5	93.5
1930	90.5	93.5	93.5	95.0	90.5	86.5	83.5	78.5	82.5	87.5	82.0	79.0
1931	72.5	73.0	76.5	79.5	75.0	74.5	72.5	68.5	71.5	76.0	77.5	73.5
1932	66.0	69.0	69.5	69.0	66.0	64.0	62.0	59.5	61.5	65.5	67.0	61.5
1933	56.5	60.5	64.5	68.0	67.0	65.5	64.5	64.5	70.5	75.5	76.5	76.5
1934	68.0	74.0	75.5	77.0	75.5	76.0	68.0	73.0	77.5	80.0	78.5	76.0
1935	72.5	73.0	74.0	75.5	77.5	75.0	70.5	71.5	74.0	81.0	82.5	78.5
1936	78.5	77.0	79.6	80.4	79.6	78.9	77.7	82.6	80.4	80.7	80.0	85.3
1937	83.4	80.7	80.0	86.7	85.3	85.6	86.4	90.2	88.3	84.5	83.4	86.0
1938	87.5	84.5	82.6	76.6	68.7	67.2	64.9	67.2	66.8	66.8	66.4	63.8
1939	71.3	72.1	74.0	67.2	78.5	83.4						

TABLE 3.6 : INDEX OF BUILDING ACTIVITY. SEASONALLY ADJUSTED
(1924 AVERAGE = 100)

	JAN	FEB	MAR	APR	MAY	JUN	JUL	AUG	SEP	OCT	NOV	DEC
1924	93.0	95.5	97.5	100.0	102.5	102.0	103.5	102.5	102.5	103.0	100.0	100.0
1925	100.0	101.5	101.5	102.0	105.5	107.0	109.5	107.0	109.5	112.0	117.0	118.5
1926	122.0	124.0	126.5	126.5	123.5	125.0	123.5	124.5	124.0	122.0	121.5	121.0
1927	119.5	120.0	117.0	116.0	117.0	118.0	117.5	118.5	117.5	118.0	117.5	118.0
1928	116.5	118.0	119.0	117.5	119.0	119.0	120.0	120.5	123.0	124.0	128.5	127.0
1929	128.5	125.5	124.5	128.5	134.0	135.0	134.5	132.5	133.0	133.5	134.5	137.0
1930	139.5	145.5	146.0	144.0	145.5	142.5	143.5	143.5	144.5	147.0	146.5	145.5
1931	143.0	143.5	144.5	142.0	137.0	136.5	138.0	137.5	134.5	128.5	125.5	124.5
1932	123.5	124.5	124.5	124.5	125.5	139.5	123.5	123.0	123.0	126.0	131.5	136.0
1933	139.5	148.0	151.5	153.5	157.5	159.5	164.5	167.5	173.0	174.5	177.0	178.0
1934	178.5	183.0	186.0	190.0	191.0	195.5	197.5	198.5	198.5	202.0	205.0	204.0
1935	206.0	209.0	213.0	216.0	221.0	217.0	219.0	222.0	226.5	228.0	233.0	238.0
1936	235.0	237.3	236.1	235.0	237.3	240.6	241.7	241.7	239.5	236.1	231.7	228.4
1937	225.1	226.2	219.6	226.2	221.8	218.5	213.0	210.8	210.8	211.9	209.7	213.0
1938	213.0	206.4	204.1	198.6	198.6	199.7	198.6	199.7	194.2	194.2	192.0	188.7
1939	182.1	183.2	185.4	186.5	181.0	178.8	174.4					

TABLE 3.7 : INDEX OF ELECTRICITY CONSUMPTION SEASONALLY ADJUSTED (1924 AVERAGE = 100)

	JAN	FEB	MAR	APR	MAY	JUN	JUL	AUG	SEP	OCT	NOV	DEC
1924	97.5	98.0	101.0	102.0	101.0	104.0	103.5	104.0	100.0	97.0	98.5	95.0
1925	97.5	98.5	98.0	99.5	100.0	98.0	100.5	102.0	101.5	99.0	100.5	99.0
1926	97.5	98.0	97.0	99.5	79.5	87.0	85.0	92.0	86.0	92.0	90.5	96.5
1927	111.5	112.0	119.0	113.0	121.0	119.0	125.5	127.5	127.5	124.0	125.0	125.0
1928	122.5	123.5	129.5	125.0	132.5	133.5	132.0	132.0	132.5	134.0	135.5	133.5
1929	142.0	148.5	138.5	144.0	141.0	144.5	147.0	148.5	143.0	148.0	152.0	141.0
1930	143.0	151.0	146.0	147.5	150.5	139.5	151.5	145.0	148.0	142.5	151.0	148.0
1931	148.0	146.5	145.5	143.5	141.5	143.5	144.0	147.0	149.5	151.0	148.5	150.0
1932	145.0	153.0	150.0	149.5	148.5	147.0	147.0	148.0	152.0	156.0	161.0	153.0
1933	158.5	157.0	152.5	152.5	160.5	155.5	163.0	164.5	169.0	168.0	181.5	183.5
1934	180.5	179.0	185.0	180.5	177.5	188.0	179.0	183.5	186.5	188.5	200.0	182.0
1935	193.0	193.0	195.0	203.0	207.0	202.5	202.0	207.0	209.0	214.0	215.0	225.0
1936	213.7	221.9	215.7	228.1	220.9	220.9	225.0	229.1	230.1	233.2	241.4	241.4
1937	238.3	238.3	256.8	250.7	253.7	251.7	252.7	257.9	255.8	255.8	264.0	270.2
1938	263.0	263.0	246.6	252.7	269.1	257.9	265.0	268.1	272.2	273.3	267.1	285.6
1939	290.7	281.5	290.7	292.8	290.7	290.7	295.9					

TABLE 3.8 : INDEX OF POSTAL RECEIPTS SEASONALLY ADJUSTED (1924 AVERAGE = 100)

	JAN	FEB	MAR	APR	MAY	JUN	JUL	AUG	SEP	OCT	NOV	DEC
1924	95.5	96.5	97.0	99.0	100.0	102.0	102.5	103.0	102.0	100.5	98.0	97.5
1925	100.5	102.5	103.0	101.5	105.5	103.5	104.0	106.0	105.0	103.0	103.0	101.5
1926	106.0	107.0	107.0	105.0	82.0	104.0	102.5	105.0	103.5	104.0	106.0	103.5
1927	108.0	108.0	108.5	109.0	112.0	108.0	110.0	111.5	111.0	110.0	110.0	107.0
1928	114.0	113.0	113.5	113.0	111.0	112.0	113.0	114.5	115.0	119.0	115.0	111.0
1929	112.0	111.0	114.0	116.0	116.0	116.0	117.5	116.5	116.0	116.0	115.5	118.5
1930	117.0	116.0	117.5	117.0	118.0	118.0	118.0	115.5	118.0	115.5	115.0	118.0
1931	116.0	117.5	120.0	115.5	116.0	119.5	115.0	115.5	114.0	113.0	117.0	116.5
1932	115.5	116.0	113.0	115.5	115.0	113.0	115.0	114.5	116.0	114.5	115.5	116.0
1933	116.0	117.0	114.5	115.0	119.0	117.0	115.5	117.0	116.5	117.5	118.0	120.5
1934	119.0	120.0	117.5	118.0	117.0	117.0	116.0	120.0	117.5	119.5	119.5	124.0
1935	120.0	121.0	117.0	123.5	120.0	118.0	120.5	121.0	124.0	122.0	123.0	127.5
1936	122.7	123.3	123.9	123.9	123.9	123.3	125.7	125.7	129.4	126.9	130.0	131.2
1937	130.6	133.6	130.6	133.6	129.4	130.0	127.5	131.8	131.8	131.2	131.8	135.4
1938	133.6	133.6	133.6	130.6	131.2	130.6	128.7	131.8	135.4	132.4	133.6	137.9
1939	136.0	135.4	135.4	130.6	130.6	134.8	131.8	134.2				

TABLE 3.9 : INDEX OF COMMERCIAL MOTOR VEHICLES IN USE SEASONALLY ADJUSTED (1924 AVERAGE = 100)

	JAN	FEB	MAR	APR	MAY	JUN	JUL	AUG	SEP	OCT	NOV	DEC
1924		94.0	95.0	96.5	97.5	99.0	100.5	102.5	103.5	104.5	105.5	105.5
1925	105.5	106.0	107.0	108.0	109.5	110.5	111.5	113.0	114.5	115.5	117.0	117.5
1926	119.0	119.5	120.0	121.0	122.5	123.5	124.5	125.5	127.0	128.0	129.0	130.5
1927	132.0	133.0	134.5	136.0	137.0	137.5	138.0	139.0	140.0	141.5	142.0	142.5
1928	143.5	144.0	145.0	145.0	146.5	147.0	148.0	148.5	149.5	151.0	151.5	152.5
1929	153.0	154.5	155.5	156.0	157.5	158.5	160.0	160.5	161.5	162.5	163.0	164.0
1930	165.0	165.5	166.0	167.0	167.5	168.0	168.5	169.0	170.0	170.5	171.5	171.0
1931	171.5	172.5	172.5	173.5	173.5	174.5	175.5	176.5	177.0	177.0	178.0	178.0
1932	177.5	178.5	179.5	180.0	181.0	180.5	180.5	180.5	181.0	181.0	181.0	182.0
1933	182.5	183.0	184.0	184.0	185.5	186.0	187.5	188.5	189.5	190.0	191.0	193.0
1934	195.0	196.5	196.5	197.5	198.0	200.0	201.5	202.5	201.5	199.5	198.0	200.0
1935	203.5	206.5	207.0	207.0	207.0	207.5	208.5	209.5	210.0	211.0	211.5	213.0
1936	215.8	216.8	217.9	217.9	219.0	220.0	220.0	221.0	222.1	224.0	225.2	226.2
1937	227.3	228.3	229.4	230.4	231.4	232.5	231.4	232.5	232.5	234.6	235.7	235.7
1938	237.7	237.7	238.7	236.6	236.6	236.6	236.6	237.7	237.7	244.0	244.0	245.0
1939	241.9	241.9	241.9	241.9								

TABLE 3.10 : INDEX OF REAL TURNOVER (1930 AVERAGE = 100)

	JAN	FEB	MAR	APR	MAY	JUN	JUL	AUG	SEP	OCT	NOV	DEC
1919	60.4	60.3	60.4	61.6	70.7	74.1	78.2	75.2	77.4	70.1	74.4	75.8
1920	75.6	75.0	78.6	71.6	67.9	68.1	69.1	66.7	67.0	65.8	66.3	65.0
1921	67.1	65.2	70.8	70.0	61.1	62.2	62.3	67.8	69.3	71.1	72.5	74.6
1922	74.6	77.4	80.2	76.9	81.3	80.2	81.3	83.2	83.2	80.8	82.2	79.6
1923	84.7	80.5	77.2	79.9	80.4	82.7	80.5	81.2	79.8	83.0	80.1	79.3
1924	77.1	81.8	79.5	82.0	82.5	85.6	85.2	83.3	87.5	83.7	81.9	84.5
1925	83.9	83.1	84.3	86.5	88.4	88.4	89.0	87.4	89.5	89.2	87.5	92.1
1926	87.1	87.5	92.5	89.5	78.1	89.3	83.7	81.4	83.6	82.7	85.9	87.6
1927	87.8	89.0	95.2	93.9	96.0	96.9	94.6	96.4	94.6	96.9	97.6	95.8
1928	95.7	98.5	98.4	95.1	100.1	99.6	96.8	99.1	97.4	99.4	98.3	97.1
1929	97.2	97.0	97.8	96.3	96.2	98.5	98.9	98.5	95.8	97.6	98.9	95.8
1930	96.7	98.1	99.0	101.1	101.9	100.2	100.9	99.3	103.4	98.4	98.4	102.6
1931	103.6	99.5	99.4	101.5	98.0	106.4	102.9	102.5	102.9	103.4	96.9	101.4
1932	101.5	102.4	104.9	104.0	98.7	104.7	104.6	104.7	101.1	100.7	103.5	106.9
1933	104.9	106.3	107.5	101.2	110.1	107.5	106.0	109.0	110.7	104.9	107.8	104.9
1934	115.2	107.6	109.4	110.5	108.8	116.6	106.3	112.6	109.3	114.1	112.2	113.2
1935	115.3	115.6	111.1	115.3	113.9	119.9	120.4	120.7	117.5	116.4	116.8	118.3
1936	120.0	124.7	117.0	118.4	120.6	121.2	123.7	120.0	125.3	125.2	122.8	127.2

4 Labour

TABLES

SOURCES

Tables 4.1–4.2 *London and Cambridge Economic Service Bulletin.*
Tables 4.3–4.7 *Ministry of Labour Gazette.*

Tables 4.8–4.9 *Ministry of Labour Gazette*; and E. H. Phelps-Brown and G. L. S. Shackle 'British Economic Fluctuations 1924–38', *Oxford Economic Papers*, II (1939), pp. 100–34.

Tables 4.10–4.16 E. H. Phelps-Brown and G. L. S. Shackle *ibid.*

WAGES

There are two monthly wage series presented here, both of which were compiled by A. L. Bowley under the auspices of the London and Cambridge Economic Service. The first, in Table 4.1, is an index of the 'unweighted average of eleven percentages, *viz.* current rates expressed as percentage of pre-war rates for Bricklayers, Bricklayers' Labourers, Compositors (Printers), Engineering Fitters, Engineering Labourers, Railwaymen, Dock Labourers, Cotton Operatives, Operatives in the Woollen and Worsted Industries, Coal-Miners, and Agricultural Labourers'.[1] Wherever possible only data representing national movements were used and in 1929, the author felt 'that these eleven composite percentages were typical of wage movements in all occupations in adequately correct proportion. They include "sheltered" and "unsheltered" trades, some industries where time-rates and others where piece-rates were common, industries predominantly skilled, predominantly unskilled or mixed, localised and scattered, town and country, some where wages moved in connection with the Cost of Living Index, and two principal women's factory industries. Under these circumstances it was considered that an unweighted average was more likely to reflect general changes . . .'[2] It was felt at the time that this unweighted average served its purpose of reflecting short-term changes in the general level of wages, without professing to show changes in earnings or to allow precise comparison of the level of wages from one year to another. The figures, in fact, make no allowance for changes in hours worked but relate to a 'normal working week' and refer only to the wholly-employed. As a general reflection of the validity of using this index as a measure of long-term changes in average wages it should be borne in mind that while the 1924 Census of Production data implied a ninety-seven per cent increase, 1914–24, the index shows only a seventy-five per cent rise.[3]

The eleven-rate index was superseded in January 1929 by the

more extensive series given in Table 4.2. Again the compiler was A. L. Bowley who made retrospective amendments on a number of occasions.[4] The series presented here is that which appeared in the *London and Cambridge Economic Service Bulletin*, converted to a 1924 base (December 1924 = 100).[5] It is a weighted index of average weekly wage-rates, not earnings. The purpose of the index was to measure alterations in wages paid to the wholly-employed for the same work over a 'normal working week', excluding overtime or short-time. The length of the 'normal working week' is thought to have changed very little during the period 1920–39, in fact.[6] The data were drawn from twenty occupational groups weighted according to 1924 Census of Production figures. These latter showed the relative size of the weekly wage-bill for each of the groups in the base period, although Bowley made additional adjustments to women's wages 'so as to give three groups, Coal, Agriculture, All Others the right proportion'.[7] The groups 'were chosen so as to include time and piece-rate payments, skilled and unskilled occupations, men and women . . .'.[8] The groups were:

1	Bricklayers	11	Local authorities
2	Bricklayers' labourers	12	Trams
3	Compositors	13	Lorry drivers
4	Dock labourers	14	Boots and shoes
5	Fitters	15	Confectionery
6	Engineering labourers	16	Tailoring
7	Shipbuilding	17	Shirtmaking
8	Railways	18	Tobacco
9	Cotton	19	Agriculture
10	Wool	20	Coal

UNEMPLOYMENT

The unemployment figures in Tables 4.3–4.7 are from two separate sources: trade union returns and National Insurance figures. They both show percentage unemployment rates.

Although the trade union returns cover only a few years in the period, their inclusion is necessary because of the inadequacy of the national insurance data up until the early 1920s. The union data provide both an alternative to the insurance figures for the years in which the two overlap, and a useful yardstick against which to judge the reliability of the main series. The figures refer only to those trade unions that offered members an unemployment insurance scheme and those making regular returns to the Ministry of Labour. As a result they cover only a minority of the labour force. They show the average percentage level of unemployment among the membership of such unions. While the unions may be considered unrepresentative in a number of important respects, especially with the bias towards skilled workers, nevertheless in 1926 the Committee on Industry and Trade believed the statistics to have been 'a sufficiently representative sample of the industrial population to justify the conclusion that the general percentages provide a valuable guide to the direction of the changes in unemployment ... although they cannot be relied upon as an absolute measure of the total amount of unemployment in all industries at any particular date'.[9]

The main unemployment series are derived from the operation of state unemployment insurance which was first introduced on a limited scale by the National Insurance Act of 1911 (the new data becoming available from September 1912). But it was not until the extension of the provisions of the 1911 Act, in 1920, that the data generated by the administration of the scheme provided a reliable measure of unemployment for a broad section of the labour force. After this extension, most of the manual and a large section of the non-manual workforce were covered by the figures, representing some eleven to twelve million of the total labour force. From 1921 until after the end of the period the data 'may be regarded as a continuous series of approximately comparable figures'.[10] The series reproduced here is the number of insured persons registered at labour exchanges as unemployed, expressed as a percentage of the total of insured workers. The count of the number of unemployed was based upon the number of insurance books lodged at the exchanges, and the reliability of the series lies in the fact that unemployed insured workers could not claim benefit unless they had registered and lodged their books at the local labour exchange.

Nevertheless, administrative changes did alter the coverage of the data during the period:

(*i*) As already noted, the major change came with the extension of the scheme in November 1920.

(*ii*) Also in September 1937 a new procedure for counting the unemployed was introduced, allowing for the exclusion from the figures of those subsequently found to have been employed on the day of the 'count'. The rate of unemployment shown by the old method was some 0.4% higher than the figures so revised and shown in the table.

(*iii*) From July 1938 the figures were extended to include groups of domestic workers for the first time. As an indication of the difference this made, on the old basis the July 1938 figure was 0.2% higher than that shown in the table.

(*iv*) From October 1931 new regulations sharply reduced the number of married women eligible for benefit, and therefore the inducement to register as unemployed.

More generally, the figures include workers attending Government training centres (not excluded until June 1940). Also included were groups of workers on short-term working, but who nevertheless qualified for benefit under the insurance scheme. Excluded are juveniles under sixteen years of age and persons insured under the Agricultural Scheme. Finally, until the end of 1921 the figures refer to Great Britain and Ireland, while from January 1922 they cover Great Britain and Northern Ireland only.[11]

Because the inclusion of workers on short-time work may make the series given in Tables 4.4 and 4.5 inappropriate for some purposes, a second series from the same source but showing the percentage of insured workers wholly unemployed, 1926–39, is reproduced in Tables 4.6 and 4.7. In all other respects the comments and qualifications relating to the broader series also apply here.

EMPLOYMENT

The data in Tables 4.8–4.16 are from E. H. Phelps-Brown and G. L. S. Shackle, 'British economic fluctuations 1924–38', *Oxford*

Economic Papers, II (1939), pp. 100–5. Their original source, however, was the Ministry of Labour.

The estimate for total insured workers employed (Tables 4.8 and 4.9) presented by Phelps-Brown and Shackle has been extended by the use of data from the Ministry's *Gazette* to cover the months up to July 1939. This series was estimated by Ministry statisticians. It refers to Great Britain only and covers insured persons aged between sixteen and sixty-four years, with allowances for those directly involved in trade disputes and absent through illness, injury, etc. As with the unemployment series it does not include those persons insured under the Agricultural Scheme or those members of the labour force not included in the National Insurance scheme. The series is only an estimate in that a count of the total number of insured workers, employed or otherwise, was taken only once a year, in July. The intervening monthly figures are Ministry estimates based on 'information which is available regarding the number of new entrants to insurance and from experience of previous years as to the proportion of the total insured population who pass outside the scope of the Acts'.[12]

Some adjustment was also made to allow for the impact of administrative changes. The number of books lodged at local labour exchanges by the unemployed insured was then deducted from the resulting estimate of total insured persons. The series for the number of insured persons unemployed has been dealt with separately above but it should be noted that it includes both the wholly unemployed and the temporarily stopped, and until September 1937 it was not adjusted to exclude those subsequently found to be employed.

While the Ministry of Labour interpolated the monthly figures between the July observations for the total insured workers employed, Phelps-Brown and Shackle performed their own interpolation for the sub-divisions shown in Tables 4.10–4.16. Their basic data were the following two series:

(*a*) 'Estimated number of insured persons, in the United Kingdom, for each trade distinguished in the Ministry of Labour classification, in July of each year.' (Phelps-Brown and Shackle, *op. cit.* p. 128). Before 1928 this included all insured persons aged sixteen and over, but from 1928 onwards was restricted to the sixteen to sixty-four groups.

(*b*) 'Total insured persons unemployed (wholly unemployed and temporarily stopped), in the United Kingdom, in each trade distinguished in the Ministry of Labour classification, on one day in each month.'

Thus, the series in Tables 4.10–4.16 refer to Great Britain and Northern Ireland, unlike those in Tables 4.8 and 4.9 which refer to Great Britain only; they also differ from Tables 4.8 and 4.9 in making no allowance for absence from work through illness, accident or trade dispute.

Phelps-Brown and Shackle used these series to estimate the number of insured persons employed in thirteen trade categories, which were subsequently regrouped to form the four broad classes shown in the tables.

Phelps-Brown and Shackle made a number of adjustments to the original data before interpolation between July figures. First, they adjusted the pre-1928 data for age differences so as to make them comparable with later figures covering the sixteen to sixty-four age group only. They also corrected the unemployment series from October 1937 on the basis of the ratio of the old to the new series as it stood in September of that year. This was an attempt to allow for the administrative changes introduced at that time which affected the inclusion of persons subsequently found to be employed. Finally, for each of the thirteen trade classes where the proportion of women was twenty-five per cent or more, they attempted to eliminate the impact of major administrative changes affecting the number of women eligible to claim insurance benefit, July 1931–July 1932.

The full list of trade groupings used by Phelps-Brown and Shackle was as follows:-

1 Employment in export-sensitive trades

Tin plate; cotton; linen; explosives; iron and steel tubes; hand tools; cutlery; saws; files; jute; woollen and worsted; musical instruments; hemp; rope; cord; twine, etc; leather tanning, currying and dressing; rubber; chemicals; pottery, earthenware, etc; scientific and photographic instruments and apparatus; shipping service.

2 Employment in durable producers' goods trades

(*a*) Metal extraction and manufacture: coke ovens and by-product works; pig-iron (blast furnaces); steel melting and iron puddling, iron and steel rolling, etc; iron ore and ironstone mining, etc; lead, tin, and copper mining; other mining and quarrying; brass; copper; tin; zinc; lead, etc; iron and steel tubes; wire netting, wire ropes.

(*b*) Engineering: general engineering; engineers' iron and steel founding; electrical engineering; marine engineering, etc; railway carriages and wagons, etc; brass and allied metal wares; metal industries not separately specified; shipbuilding and ship repairing; electrical wiring and contracting; electrical cable, apparatus, lamps, etc.

3 Employment in durable consumers' goods trades

(*a*) Mineral materials: stone quarrying and mining; slate quarrying and mining; clay, sand, gravel and chalk pits; artificial stone and concrete etc; cement, lime-kilns and whiting; brick, tile, pipe making, etc.

(*b*) Manufactured materials: glass (excluding bottles and scientific glass); paint, varnish, red lead, etc; stone, grate, pipe, etc, and general iron founding; heating and ventilating apparatus.

(*c*) Building: (no allowance was made for separating out commercial and industrial premises).

(*d*) Motor vehicles, cycles and aircraft: (despite the obvious anomaly of including aircraft in this category no adjustment was made).

(*e*) Timber and furnishings: sawmilling and machined woodwork; furniture making, upholstering, etc; other woodworking; matt-paper making; carpets; oilcloth, linoleum, etc.

4 Employment in non-durable consumer and consumer services trades

(*a*) Silk and artificial silk: silk spinning and manufacture and artificial silk weaving, etc; artificial silk yarn manufacture.

(*b*) Clothing: linen; hosiery; lace; tailoring; dressmaking and millinery; hats and caps; shirts, collars, underclothing, etc; other dress industries; boots, shoes, slippers and clogs; leather tanning, currying and dressing; leather goods.

(*c*) Food, drink and tobacco: bread, biscuits, cakes, etc; grain milling; cocoa, chocolate and sugar confectionary; other food industries; drink industries; tobacco, cigars, cigarettes and snuff.

(*d*) Miscellaneous consumers' goods: paper and paper boards; printing, publishing, and bookbinding; brushes and brooms; toys, games and sports requisites; musical instruments; watches, clocks, plate, jewellery, etc.

(*e*) Distribution and services: distributive trades; entertainments, sport, etc; hotel, public house, restaurant, boarding house, club, etc., service; laundry service.

NOTES

1 A. L. Bowley, *A New Index-Number of Wages*, London and Cambridge Economic Service Special Memorandum 28 (London, 1929), p. 1.

2 *Ibid.*, p. 2.

3 A. L. Bowley 'Index numbers of wage-rates and cost of living' *JRSS*, series A, CXV, part IV (1952), p. 501.

4 *Ibid.*, pp. 500–6; and LCES Special Memorandum 28 *op. cit.*; J. A. Dowie, '1919–20 is in need of attention' *Economic History Review*, series 2, XXVIII (1975), pp. 429–50 discussed the series in detail.

5 In the original form the 1925–8 data were on a July 1914 base.

6 Bowley believed that while there was a general reduction of 5–6 hours per week in 1919–20, very few general changes occurred thereafter until 1948. See LCES Special Memorandum 50 (1947), p. 5; and Dowie *op. cit.* pp. 438–41.

7 LCES Special Memorandum 18, *op. cit.*, p. 6.

8 *JRSS* (1952), *op. cit.*, p. 500.

9 *Survey of Industrial Relations, 1926*, Committee on Industry and Trade (London, HMSO, 1926), pp. 218–9.

10 Department of Employment and Productivity *British Labour Statistics: Historical Abstract 1886–1968* (London, 1971), p. 16; W. R. Garside, *The Measurement of Unemployment* (Oxford, 1980), especially Chapter 2, discusses coverage of the main series in some detail.

11 No figure is given for October 1920 because of the coal dispute of that month.

12 *Ministry of Labour Gazette*, XXXVII (October 1929), p. 357.

TABLE 4.1 : INDEX OF 11 WEEKLY WAGE RATES (JULY 1914 = 100)

	JAN	FEB	MAR	APR	MAY	JUN	JUL	AUG	SEP	OCT	NOV	DEC
1919	206	206	207	207	209	210	216	216	218	218	220	226
1920	229	229	234	235	253	261	264	266	270	270	274	276
1921	277	276	275	271	269	264	253	243	237	233	227	223
1922	217	214	214	206	202	197	194	191	181	180	179	178
1923	177	177	177	177	177	176	174	174	174	174	173	173
1924	173	174	176	176	177	179	179	179	179	179	179	179
1925	180	181	181	181	181	181	180	180	180	180	180	180
1926	180	180	180	180	180	180	180	180	180	180	180	181
1927	181	181	181	181	181	181	180	181	181	181	181	181
1928	181	181	180	180	180	180						

TABLE 4.2 : INDEX OF AVERAGE WEEKLY WAGES (1924 AVERAGE = 100)

	JAN	FEB	MAR	APR	MAY	JUN	JUL	AUG	SEP	OCT	NOV	DEC
1925	100.5	100.8	100.8	101.0	101.0	100.5	100.5	100.5	100.5	100.5	100.5	100.5
1926	100.5	100.5	100.5	100.5	100.5	100.5	100.5	100.5	100.5	100.5	100.5	101.0
1927	101.3	101.0	101.0	101.0	100.5	100.5	100.0	100.8	100.8	100.5	100.5	100.5
1928	100.5	100.0	99.7	99.7	99.7	99.7	99.7	99.5	99.5	99.5	99.5	99.5
1929	99.5	99.5	99.5	99.5	99.5	99.5	99.5	99.5	99.0	99.0	99.0	99.0
1930	99.0	98.5	98.5	98.5	98.2	98.2	98.2	98.2	98.2	98.2	98.2	98.2
1931	98.0	97.5	97.5	97.0	97.0	97.0	97.0	96.8	96.8	96.5	96.5	96.5
1932	96.0	95.5	95.5	95.5	95.5	95.5	95.2	95.2	95.2	95.0	94.5	94.5
1933	94.5	94.0	94.0	94.0	94.0	94.0	94.0	94.0	94.0	94.0	94.0	94.0
1934	94.0	94.0	94.0	94.0	94.0	94.0	94.0	94.0	94.0	94.2	94.2	94.2
1935	94.2	94.2	94.2	94.2	94.7	94.7	95.7	95.7	95.7	95.7	95.7	95.7
1936	96.0	97.0	97.0	97.0	97.0	97.2	98.0	98.0	98.0	98.0	98.0	98.0
1937	99.0	100.0	100.0	100.2	100.7	100.7	101.0	101.2	101.7	102.2	103.0	103.0
1938	103.2	104.0	104.0	104.5	104.5	104.5	104.5	104.5	104.5	104.5	104.5	104.5
1939	105.0	105.0	105.0	105.0	105.0	105.8	105.8	105.8	106.0	106.0	107.7	109.2

TABLE 4.3 : PERCENTAGE OF TRADE UNIONISTS UNEMPLOYED

	JAN	FEB	MAR	APR	MAY	JUN	JUL	AUG	SEP	OCT	NOV	DEC
1919	2.4	2.8	2.8	2.7	2.1	1.7	2.0	2.2	1.6	2.6	2.9	3.2
1920	2.9	1.6	1.1	0.9	1.1	1.2	1.4	1.6	2.2	5.3	3.7	6.0
1921	7.1	8.7	10.2	15.1	19.9	20.6	16.9	16.6	15.0	15.7	16.1	16.2
1922	16.5	16.2	16.2	16.8	16.2	15.5	14.5	14.1	14.4	14.0	14.2	13.8
1923	13.6	12.9	12.2	11.2	11.2	11.0	10.9	11.1	10.9	10.5	10.2	9.3
1924	8.5	8.2	7.8	7.5	7.0	7.2	7.4	7.9	8.6	8.7	8.6	9.2
1925	9.0	9.4	9.0	9.4	10.1	12.3	11.2	11.4	11.4	11.3	11.0	11.0
1926	10.6	10.4	10.1	10.0	13.2	12.9	13.2	13.3	13.6	13.6	13.2	12.2

TABLE 4.4 : PERCENTAGE OF INSURED WORKERS UNEMPLOYED

	JAN	FEB	MAR	APR	MAY	JUN	JUL	AUG	SEP	OCT	NOV	DEC
1920	6.1	4.4	3.6	2.8	2.7	2.6	2.7	2.9	3.8	3.6	3.5	7.9
1921	11.2	13.1	15.4	20.2	23.4	22.4	17.9	15.6	14.2	14.5	17.2	18.0
1922	17.7	17.1	16.0	15.9	14.6	13.7	13.1	12.8	12.7	12.6	13.0	12.8
1923	13.3	12.4	11.7	11.5	11.2	11.3	11.6	11.8	11.7	11.7	11.5	10.6
1924	11.9	10.6	9.8	9.7	9.4	9.3	9.8	10.5	10.6	10.9	10.8	10.7
1925	11.2	11.3	11.1	10.9	10.9	11.9	11.2	12.1	12.0	11.4	11.0	10.4
1926	11.0	10.4	9.8	9.1	14.3	14.6	14.4	14.0	13.7	13.6	13.5	11.9
1927	12.0	10.9	9.8	9.4	8.7	8.8	9.2	9.3	9.3	9.5	9.9	9.8
1928	10.7	10.4	9.5	9.5	9.8	10.7	11.6	11.5	11.3	11.7	12.1	11.1
1929	12.2	12.1	10.0	9.8	9.7	9.6	9.7	9.9	9.9	10.3	10.9	11.0
1930	12.4	12.9	13.7	14.2	15.0	15.4	16.7	17.0	17.5	18.5	18.9	19.9
1931	21.1	21.3	21.0	20.4	20.3	21.2	21.9	21.9	22.4	21.7	21.2	20.7
1932	22.2	21.9	20.8	21.3	22.0	22.2	22.8	23.0	22.8	21.9	22.2	21.6
1933	23.0	22.7	21.9	21.3	20.4	19.4	19.5	19.1	18.4	18.1	17.9	17.5
1934	18.6	18.1	17.2	16.6	16.2	16.4	16.7	16.5	16.0	16.3	16.3	16.0
1935	17.6	17.5	16.4	15.6	15.5	15.4	15.2	14.9	14.9	14.5	14.5	14.1
1936	16.2	15.3	14.2	13.6	12.8	12.8	12.4	12.0	12.1	12.0	12.0	12.0
1937	12.4	12.0	11.6	10.5	10.7	10.0	10.1	9.9	9.7	10.1	10.9	12.1
1938	13.2	13.1	12.7	12.7	12.8	13.2	12.9	12.6	12.8	12.7	13.0	12.9
1939	14.2	13.3	12.2	11.5	10.5	9.6	9.0	8.7	9.1	9.6	9.5	9.1

TABLE 4.5 : PERCENTAGE OF INSURED WORKERS UNEMPLOYED.
SEASONALLY ADJUSTED

	JAN	FEB	MAR	APR	MAY	JUN	JUL	AUG	SEP	OCT	NOV	DEC
1920	5.4	4.1	3.4	2.6	2.6	2.5	2.9	3.1	4.0	4.0	3.8	7.8
1921	10.0	12.1	14.7	18.8	22.2	21.6	19.4	16.9	15.1	15.9	18.9	17.7
1922	15.8	15.8	15.3	14.8	13.9	13.2	14.2	13.9	13.5	13.8	14.3	12.6
1923	11.9	11.5	11.2	10.7	10.6	10.9	12.6	12.8	12.5	12.8	12.6	10.4
1924	10.6	9.8	9.4	9.0	8.9	9.0	10.6	11.4	11.3	12.0	11.9	10.5
1925	10.0	10.4	10.6	10.2	10.3	11.5	12.2	13.1	12.8	12.5	12.1	10.2
1926	10.5	10.2	10.4	9.9	14.6	14.6	14.0	13.7	13.5	13.4	13.2	12.0
1927	11.5	10.7	10.4	10.2	8.9	8.8	8.9	9.1	9.2	9.4	9.6	9.9
1928	10.2	10.2	10.1	10.3	10.0	10.7	11.3	11.2	11.2	11.5	11.8	11.2
1929	11.7	11.9	10.6	10.6	9.9	9.6	9.4	9.7	9.8	10.2	10.6	11.1
1930	11.8	12.7	14.5	15.4	15.3	15.4	16.2	16.6	17.3	18.3	18.4	20.1
1931	20.2	21.0	22.2	22.1	20.7	21.2	21.3	21.4	22.1	21.4	20.7	20.9
1932	21.2	21.6	22.0	23.1	22.4	22.2	22.2	22.5	22.5	21.6	21.6	21.8
1933	20.7	20.8	21.1	21.4	20.9	20.2	20.0	19.9	19.2	18.8	18.1	17.5
1934	16.7	16.6	16.6	16.7	16.6	17.1	17.1	17.2	16.7	16.9	16.5	16.0
1935	15.8	16.1	15.8	15.7	15.9	16.1	15.6	15.5	15.6	15.0	14.7	14.1
1936	14.6	14.0	13.7	13.7	13.1	13.4	12.7	12.5	12.6	12.4	12.1	12.0
1937	11.1	11.0	11.2	10.5	11.0	10.4	10.4	10.3	10.1	10.5	11.0	12.1
1938	11.9	12.0	12.3	12.8	13.1	13.8	13.2	13.1	13.4	13.2	13.2	12.9
1939	12.8	12.2	11.8	11.6	10.8	10.0	9.2	9.1	9.5	9.9	9.6	9.1

TABLE 4.6 : PERCENTAGE OF INSURED WORKERS WHOLLY UNEMPLOYED

	JAN	FEB	MAR	APR	MAY	JUN	JUL	AUG	SEP	OCT	NOV	DEC
1926	9.2	8.7	8.2	7.6	8.7	9.0	8.9	9.0	9.0	9.3	9.4	9.1
1927	9.4	8.7	7.8	7.1	6.6	6.5	6.6	6.8	6.9	7.2	7.6	7.7
1928	8.3	8.2	7.6	7.6	7.5	7.7	8.1	8.2	8.6	8.9	9.3	9.1
1929	9.7	9.6	8.3	7.8	7.5	7.3	7.3	7.6	7.8	8.2	8.8	8.9
1930	9.7	9.9	10.4	10.6	10.8	10.8	11.3	12.1	12.7	13.9	14.8	14.9
1931	16.5	16.7	16.5	16.3	16.3	16.0	16.3	16.7	17.4	18.1	18.0	17.7
1932	18.4	18.2	17.5	17.3	17.1	16.7	17.1	17.3	17.8	17.9	18.2	18.1
1933	18.9	18.7	18.0	17.2	16.6	15.8	15.5	15.3	15.3	15.3	15.3	15.1
1934	15.8	15.4	14.7	14.0	13.5	12.9	12.8	12.9	13.3	13.7	13.9	13.8
1935	14.9	14.7	14.0	13.4	13.1	12.5	12.2	12.3	12.6	12.6	12.8	12.5
1936	13.5	13.3	12.4	11.7	11.0	10.5	10.2	10.2	10.4	10.5	10.6	10.6
1937	11.0	10.8	10.4	9.6	9.1	8.5	8.3	8.4	8.4	8.9	9.4	9.8
1938	10.7	10.7	10.4	10.2	10.0	9.9	9.8	9.7	10.1	10.5	10.8	10.8
1939	11.6	11.3	10.6	9.9	9.2	8.3	7.7	7.3	7.6	8.7	8.5	8.1

TABLE 4.7 : PERCENTAGE OF INSURED WORKERS WHOLLY UNEMPLOYED. SEASONALLY ADJUSTED

	JAN	FEB	MAR	APR	MAY	JUN	JUL	AUG	SEP	OCT	NOV	DEC
1926	8.4	8.1	8.2	7.8	9.2	9.7	9.5	9.4	9.1	9.1	8.9	8.8
1927	8.6	8.1	7.8	7.3	7.0	7.0	7.0	7.1	7.0	7.0	7.2	7.4
1928	7.6	7.6	7.6	7.8	8.0	8.3	8.6	8.5	8.7	8.7	8.8	8.8
1929	8.8	8.9	8.3	8.0	8.0	7.9	7.8	7.9	7.9	8.0	8.3	8.6
1930	8.8	9.2	10.3	10.9	11.5	11.7	12.0	12.6	12.9	13.6	14.0	14.3
1931	15.0	15.6	16.4	16.8	17.3	17.3	17.3	17.4	17.7	17.7	17.0	17.0
1932	16.8	17.0	17.4	17.8	18.1	18.1	18.2	18.0	18.1	17.5	17.2	17.4
1933	16.9	16.9	17.0	17.0	17.1	17.1	16.8	16.4	16.0	15.5	15.1	14.8
1934	14.2	13.9	13.9	13.9	13.9	14.0	13.8	13.8	13.9	13.9	13.7	13.5
1935	13.3	13.3	13.2	13.3	13.5	13.6	13.2	13.2	13.2	12.8	12.6	12.2
1936	12.1	12.0	11.7	11.6	11.3	11.4	11.0	10.9	10.9	10.7	10.5	10.4
1937	9.9	9.7	9.8	9.5	9.4	9.2	9.0	9.0	8.8	9.0	9.3	9.6
1938	9.6	9.7	9.8	10.1	10.3	10.7	10.6	10.4	10.6	10.7	10.6	10.6
1939	10.4	10.2	10.0	9.8	9.5	9.0	8.3	7.8	7.9	8.8	8.4	7.9

TABLE 4.8 : INSURED WORKERS IN EMPLOYMENT (THOUSANDS).

	JAN	FEB	MAR	APR	MAY	JUN	JUL	AUG	SEP	OCT	NOV	DEC
1924	9247	9343	9514	9596	9634	9656	9539	9547	9550	9535	9559	9591
1925	9555	9565	9602	9646	9662	9564	9468	9528	9575	9658	9705	9798
1926	9732	9811	9893	9983	8361	8355	8396	8468	8555	8690	8833	9670
1927	9721	9855	9978	10043	10123	10116	10077	10069	10083	10059	10015	10039
1928	9966	10005	10113	10128	10104	9988	9942	9971	10020	9981	9939	10071
1929	9949	9971	10223	10259	10271	10301	10308	10304	10316	10278	10231	10225
1930	10076	10029	9993	9922	9857	9861	9746	9734	9691	9593	9576	9487
1931	9227	9338	9395	9494	9528	9438	9346	9377	9338	9448	9522	9605
1932	9361	9385	9517	9442	9351	9331	9251	9206	9144	9388	9359	9440
1933	9265	9316	9414	9502	9617	9744	9743	9795	9883	9927	9960	10011
1934	9878	9945	10061	10145	10193	10173	10147	10180	10246	10213	10222	10259
1935	10067	10097	10219	10341	10359	10391	10414	10461	10483	10504	10560	10629
1936	10391	10525	10689	10785	10918	10933	11011	11091	11110	11141	11166	11182
1937	11163	11250	11310	11472	11473	11613	11623	11672	11663	11620	11537	11401
1938	11276	11295	11356	11369	11363	11326	11370	11404	11386	11412	11385	11409
1939	11242	11376	11542	11641	11793	11925						

TABLE 4.9 : INSURED WORKERS IN EMPLOYMENT (THOUSANDS)
SEASONALLY ADJUSTED

	JAN	FEB	MAR	APR	MAY	JUN	JUL	AUG	SEP	OCT	NOV	DEC
1924	9306	9361	9449	9490	9640	9677	9591	9584	9580	9546	9568	9520
1925	9616	9584	9537	9539	9668	9585	9520	9565	9605	9669	9714	9725
1926	9794	9830	9826	9872	8366	8373	8442	8501	8582	8700	8841	9598
1927	9783	9874	9910	9932	10129	10138	10132	10108	10114	10071	10024	9965
1928	10029	10024	10044	10016	10110	10009	9997	10010	10051	9993	9948	9996
1929	10012	9990	10153	10145	10277	10323	10365	10344	10348	10290	10241	10149
1930	10140	10048	9925	9812	9863	9882	9800	9772	9721	9604	9585	9417
1931	9286	9356	9331	9389	9534	9458	9397	9413	9367	9459	9531	9534
1932	9421	9403	9452	9337	9357	9351	9302	9242	9173	9399	9368	9370
1933	9324	9334	9350	9397	9623	9765	9797	9833	9914	9939	9969	9937
1934	9941	9964	9993	10032	10199	10195	10203	10219	10278	10225	10232	10183
1935	10131	10117	10149	10226	10365	10413	10471	10501	10516	10516	10570	10550
1936	10457	10545	10616	10665	10925	10956	11072	11134	11145	11154	11176	11099
1937	11234	11272	11233	11345	11480	11638	11687	11717	11699	11633	11548	11317
1938	11348	11317	11279	11243	11370	11350	11433	11448	11422	11425	11396	11325
1939	11314	11398	11464	11512	11800	11950						

TABLE 4.10 : INSURED WORKERS EMPLOYED IN EXPORT SENSITIVE TRADES (THOUSANDS)

	JAN	FEB	MAR	APR	MAY	JUN	JUL	AUG	SEP	OCT	NOV	DEC
1924	1295	1303	1309	1309	1302	1301	1319	1289	1301	1317	1328	1323
1925	1323	1315	1316	1300	1298	1291	1262	1272	1310	1334	1338	1341
1926	1329	1330	1335	1332	1134	1114	1105	1163	1191	1227	1240	1303
1927	1324	1356	1378	1373	1374	1369	1353	1353	1362	1357	1350	1360
1928	1350	1359	1371	1363	1347	1323	1300	1298	1306	1313	1322	1338
1929	1326	1333	1344	1339	1335	1333	1325	1324	1338	1336	1326	1321
1930	1265	1238	1205	1180	1131	1101	1066	1054	1057	1069	1062	979
1931	998	1012	1049	1047	1046	1021	988	989	977	1083	1129	1138
1932	1120	1130	1145	1116	1041	1045	1020	1024	1049	1111	1114	1112
1933	1096	1101	1095	1075	1107	1134	1127	1140	1167	1174	1178	1175
1934	1147	1148	1155	1143	1143	1129	1097	1107	1131	1137	1137	1131
1935	1107	1106	1109	1114	1112	1116	1103	1114	1120	1141	1146	1151
1936	1132	1138	1145	1144	1149	1146	1151	1157	1168	1179	1185	1190
1937	1194	1202	1208	1211	1199	1210	1189	1203	1198	1194	1161	1134
1938	1089	1081	1070	1059	1033	1040	1033	1034	1047	1089		

TABLE 4.11 : INSURED WORKERS EMPLOYED IN EXPORT SENSITIVE TRADES. (THOUSANDS) SEASONALLY ADJUSTED

	JAN	FEB	MAR	APR	MAY	JUN	JUL	AUG	SEP	OCT	NOV	DEC
1924	1274	1277	1275	1283	1399	1404	1339	1300	1296	1286	1292	1288
1925	1302	1288	1282	1274	1395	1394	1281	1283	1305	1303	1301	1306
1926	1308	1303	1300	1306	1219	1203	1122	1173	1187	1198	1206	1269
1927	1303	1328	1342	1346	1476	1478	1374	1365	1357	1325	1313	1324
1928	1328	1331	1335	1336	1447	1428	1320	1310	1301	1282	1286	1303
1929	1305	1306	1309	1313	1435	1439	1345	1336	1333	1305	1290	1286
1930	1245	1213	1174	1157	1215	1188	1082	1063	1053	1044	1033	953
1931	982	991	1022	1026	1124	1102	1003	998	974	1058	1098	1108
1932	1102	1107	1115	1094	1119	1128	1035	1033	1045	1085	1084	1083
1933	1078	1079	1066	1054	1190	1224	1144	1150	1163	1147	1146	1144
1934	1129	1125	1125	1120	1228	1219	1114	1117	1127	1110	1106	1101
1935	1089	1084	1080	1092	1195	1205	1120	1124	1116	1114	1115	1121
1936	1114	1115	1115	1121	1235	1237	1168	1167	1164	1151	1153	1159
1937	1175	1178	1176	1187	1288	1306	1207	1214	1194	1166	1129	1104
1938	1071	1059	1042	1038	1110	1123	1049	1043	1043	1064		

TABLE 4.12 : INSURED WORKERS EMPLOYED IN PRODUCER DURABLE GOODS INDUSTRIES. (THOUSANDS)

	JAN	FEB	MAR	APR	MAY	JUN	JUL	AUG	SEP	OCT	NOV	DEC
1924	1401	1436	1446	1433	1445	1443	1439	1418	1411	1410	1416	1413
1925	1417	1421	1420	1416	1430	1422	1418	1411	1412	1415	1415	1418
1926	1411	1416	1419	1429	1250	1238	1245	1239	1242	1236	1236	1312
1927	1375	1409	1431	1440	1456	1456	1457	1452	1452	1450	1445	1447
1928	1454	1455	1451	1447	1447	1437	1427	1429	1436	1436	1435	1454
1929	1450	1461	1485	1492	1493	1500	1499	1493	1493	1502	1488	1493
1930	1474	1466	1447	1430	1428	1411	1390	1356	1330	1296	1270	1229
1931	1218	1196	1173	1169	1163	1154	1147	1132	1116	1135	1139	1146
1932	1121	1120	1130	1122	1100	1105	1095	1093	1091	1095	1090	1099
1933	1106	1075	1088	1096	1129	1154	1162	1175	1198	1213	1234	1252
1934	1242	1254	1273	1296	1312	1327	1332	1334	1342	1349	1354	1360
1935	1346	1349	1359	1369	1400	1389	1398	1412	1420	1436	1454	1468
1936	1463	1478	1500	1519	1540	1558	1566	1584	1605	1627	1644	1656
1937	1669	1686	1698	1722	1735	1759	1767	1775	1783	1785	1782	1774
1938	1759	1757	1755	1754	1751	1737	1742	1742	1738	1759		

TABLE 4.13 : INSURED WORKERS EMPLOYED IN CONSUMER DURABLE GOODS INDUSTRIES. (THOUSANDS)

	JAN	FEB	MAR	APR	MAY	JUN	JUL	AUG	SEP	OCT	NOV	DEC
1924	1194	1222	1249	1262	1271	1275	1262	1254	1265	1267	1259	1273
1925	1266	1284	1307	1322	1336	1342	1338	1341	1343	1343	1340	1329
1926	1323	1352	1386	1404	1343	1347	1351	1359	1363	1361	1357	1378
1927	1374	1406	1443	1465	1483	1486	1481	1476	1462	1447	1431	1410
1928	1391	1412	1452	1462	1473	1463	1459	1459	1460	1454	1442	1443
1929	1394	1347	1469	1498	1513	1518	1519	1510	1499	1481	1456	1448
1930	1422	1420	1437	1455	1466	1458	1438	1431	1422	1405	1375	1360
1931	1306	1314	1349	1385	1401	1394	1387	1372	1357	1333	1312	1297
1932	1244	1248	1290	1308	1306	1308	1292	1293	1292	1292	1284	1281
1933	1221	1249	1328	1381	1421	1430	1430	1447	1458	1472	1470	1435
1934	1429	1465	1504	1547	1573	1583	1572	1577	1577	1578	1566	1561
1935	1514	1550	1607	1635	1650	1661	1666	1674	1674	1682	1674	1671
1936	1560	1653	1727	1766	1800	1805	1806	1816	1818	1817	1804	1778
1937	1777	1802	1808	1871	1883	1903	1900	1902	1908	1902	1878	1797
1938	1803	1826	1870	1893	1903	1898	1890	1903	1896	1883		

TABLE 4.14 : INSURED WORKERS EMPLOYED IN CONSUMER DURABLE GOODS INDUSTRIES. (THOUSANDS) SEASONALLY ADJUSTED

	JAN	FEB	MAR	APR	MAY	JUN	JUL	AUG	SEP	OCT	NOV	DEC
1924	1246	1260	1250	1241	1245	1249	1244	1239	1254	1263	1269	1294
1925	1321	1324	1308	1300	1308	1314	1319	1325	1331	1339	1351	1351
1926	1381	1394	1387	1381	1315	1319	1332	1343	1351	1357	1368	1401
1927	1434	1450	1444	1441	1452	1455	1460	1458	1449	1443	1443	1433
1928	1452	1456	1453	1438	1442	1433	1438	1441	1447	1450	1454	1467
1929	1455	1389	1470	1474	1482	1487	1497	1492	1486	1477	1468	1472
1930	1484	1464	1438	1431	1436	1428	1418	1414	1410	1401	1386	1382
1931	1363	1355	1350	1362	1372	1365	1367	1356	1345	1329	1323	1318
1932	1298	1287	1291	1287	1279	1281	1274	1277	1281	1288	1295	1302
1933	1274	1288	1329	1359	1391	1400	1410	1430	1445	1468	1482	1458
1934	1491	1511	1505	1522	1540	1550	1550	1558	1563	1573	1579	1586
1935	1580	1598	1608	1608	1616	1627	1642	1654	1659	1677	1688	1698
1936	1628	1705	1729	1737	1763	1768	1780	1794	1802	1812	1819	1807
1937	1855	1858	1810	1841	1844	1864	1873	1879	1891	1896	1894	1826
1938	1882	1883	1872	1864	1864	1859	1863	1856	1879	1877		

TABLE 4.15 : INSURED WORKERS EMPLOYED IN CONSUMER NON-DURABLE GOODS INDUSTRIES. (THOUSANDS)

	JAN	FEB	MAR	APR	MAY	JUN	JUL	AUG	SEP	OCT	NOV	DEC
1924	3141	3171	3202	3226	3254	3278	3289	3280	3275	3270	3265	3281
1925	3263	3283	3311	3333	3363	3389	3393	3391	3394	3404	3397	3428
1926	3406	3434	3467	3499	3401	3437	3437	3440	3450	3455	3464	3502
1927	3495	3525	3570	3605	3634	3648	3650	3641	3648	3651	3645	3665
1928	3631	3646	3677	3691	3693	3680	3681	3696	3699	3702	3689	3712
1929	3680	3703	3751	3776	3797	3809	3818	3809	3810	3802	3786	3795
1930	3744	3741	3743	3756	3778	3792	3781	3772	3753	3744	3727	3720
1931	3671	3692	3735	3777	3793	3818	3808	3809	3789	3801	3831	3870
1932	3825	3848	3894	3901	3893	3911	3895	3895	3896	3912	3894	3919
1933	3857	3872	3903	3953	3999	4052	4054	4059	4057	4059	4057	4080
1934	4006	4026	4065	4097	4118	4132	4119	4107	4099	4087	4072	4087
1935	4004	4017	4052	4094	4109	4131	4136	4122	4117	4128	4115	4149
1936	4080	4101	4146	4189	4229	4256	4272	4276	4266	4264	4251	4271
1937	4232	4252	4285	4328	4340	4381	4386	4388	4406	4377	4340	4341
1938	4274	4289	4310	4338	4367	4379	4401	4419	4421	4388		

TABLE 4.16 : INSURED WORKERS EMPLOYED IN CONSUMER NON-DURABLE GOODS INDUSTRIES. (THOUSANDS) SEASONALLY ADJUSTED

	JAN	FEB	MAR	APR	MAY	JUN	JUL	AUG	SEP	OCT	NOV	DEC
1924	3182	3203	3210	3214	3239	3251	3267	3267	3271	3270	3277	3280
1925	3306	3316	3319	3321	3348	3361	3371	3377	3390	3404	3409	3427
1926	3451	3468	3476	3486	3386	3408	3414	3426	3445	3455	3476	3501
1927	3541	3560	3579	3592	3618	3618	3626	3626	3643	3651	3658	3664
1928	3679	3682	3686	3678	3676	3649	3657	3681	3694	3702	3702	3711
1929	3729	3740	3760	3762	3780	3777	3793	3794	3805	3802	3800	3794
1930	3793	3778	3752	3742	3761	3760	3756	3757	3748	3744	3740	3719
1931	3719	3729	3744	3763	3776	3786	3783	3794	3784	3801	3845	3869
1932	3875	3886	3904	3887	3876	3878	3869	3879	3891	3912	3908	3918
1933	3908	3910	3913	3939	3981	4018	4027	4043	4052	4059	4072	4078
1934	4059	4066	4075	4082	4100	4097	4092	4091	4094	4087	4087	4085
1935	4057	4057	4062	4079	4091	4096	4109	4105	4112	4128	4130	4147
1936	4134	4142	4156	4174	4210	4220	4244	4259	4260	4264	4266	4269
1937	4288	4294	4296	4312	4321	4344	4357	4370	4400	4377	4356	4339
1938	4331	4331	4321	4322	4348	4342	4372	4401	4415	4388		

5 Overseas Trade and Shipping

TABLES

SOURCES

Tables 5.1–5.20 and Tables 5.23–5.26 *Accounts relating to the Trade and Navigation of the United Kingdom* (monthly)

Tables 5.21, 5.22 *The Economist*

There are twenty-six series in this section, twenty monthly trade series and six shipping series covering the years 1919/1920–39. The principal series are the monthly values of the United Kingdom's merchandise trade and U.K. exports (f.o.b.) and total imports (c.i.f.) given in aggregate and disaggregate form, i.e., in total and by *Trade Account* classification, the principal classes being Classes I, II and III representing:

I Food, drink and tobacco

II Raw materials, and articles mainly unmanufactured

III Articles wholly or mainly manufactured

The total figure includes the miscellaneous and generally tiny items of Classes IV and V, 'animals not for food' and 'parcel post' respectively. The figures are given in 'raw', seasonally adjusted, and constant price form.

The series of most interest to economists and economic historians are retained imports and domestic exports. Re-exports were once of great significance in British trade but ever since the early nineteenth century they have been in relative decline. At the end of the nineteenth century they were of the order of twenty-five per cent of domestic exports whereas by the end of the 1930s they had fallen to less than half that figure, at a time when exports themselves had fallen in significance.

The three other series that are included here are not strictly trade, but are closely associated, and most conveniently included in this section. *The Economist* index of shipping freight was based on a daily average of the shipping tonnage engaged in overseas trade, entered and cleared at ports in the United Kingdom.

The two other series were produced by the Board of Trade. Again they are monthly series of shipping tonnage entering and leaving British ports with cargoes during that month shown.

There is no need to dwell on the great price changes that took place between the Wars, and already mentioned in the introduction. Suffice to say that for some purposes there is an obvious need to present the trade series with the price effect removed and where appropriate this has been done. The data are given in 1924 prices. In converting to constant prices an attempt has been made to use the most appropriate price series rather than simply a general one for each series. The following list shows which price series was used to carry out the adjustment in each trade series.

Trade series	**Price index**
Exports	
Class I Food etc.	B.o.T. wholesale price index: Food
Class II Raw materials	B.o.T. wholesale price index: Materials
Class III Manufactures etc.	B.o.T. wholesale price index: General
Total	B.o.T. wholesale price index: General
Imports	
Class I Food etc.	B.o.T. wholesale price index: Food
Class II Raw materials	B.o.T. wholesale price index: Materials
Class III Manufactures etc.	B.o.T. wholesale price index: General
Total	B.o.T. wholesale price index: General

The other statistical problem with the series is the presence of seasonality. Most series in this grouping did in fact exhibit a seasonal pattern, the chief exceptions being exports and imports of manufactures and exports of raw materials. None of these is particularly surprising. Raw material exports were dominated by coal thus there is little reason to expect seasonality and none was found. Of course, although the production of food and some raw materials are seasonally determined it does not follow that either

Class I or Class II imports would exhibit a seasonal pattern, since different sources of supply frequently served to even out the flow and reduce or even eliminate any seasonal pattern. However, as it happened, all the other trade series had to be deseasonalised (using the method described in the introduction) and the adjusted data are presented.

As mentioned in the general introduction, a major change, affecting primarily the trade series, was that of the creation of the Irish Free State. Prior to April 1923 the trade of this territory was included in the trade of the United Kingdom. From April, the trade of the area, 'in so far as it is carried on with the United Kingdom . . . appears in the trade accounts as overseas trade between the United Kingdom and a British country'.[1] A rough measure of the effect of this is that for the years following division the United Kingdom's imports were higher by around four per cent than they would have been without this division of Ireland, exports were higher by some five per cent and re-exports were greater by around eight per cent.[2] Care should therefore be taken to allow for this change when using the figures over the whole period. Apart from this the trade accounts are very consistent, there being no major changes of commodity classification or in definition or presentation[3] over the entire inter-war period.

NOTES

1 G. W. Daniels, 'Recent changes in the overseas trade of the United Kingdom', *Transactions of the Manchester Statistical Society 1930–31*.

2 *Ibid.*, p. 2.

3 J. Stafford, J. M. Maten and Muriel Venning, 'The United Kingdom', p. 293, in R. G. D. Allen and J. Edwardy Ely (eds) *International Trade Statistics* (Chapman and Hall, 1953).

TABLE 5.1 : EXPORTS OF U.K. GOODS (F.O.B.) : FOOD,DRINK AND TOBACCO.
(£ MILLIONS)

	JAN	FEB	MAR	APR	MAY	JUN	JUL	AUG	SEP	OCT	NOV	DEC
1919	1.4	1.3	1.8	2.9	3.3	2.7	2.6	2.6	2.9	3.8	4.3	4.3
1920	4.8	3.9	4.3	4.0	4.0	4.3	4.5	3.5	4.3	4.7	4.7	3.8
1921	3.9	3.1	2.9	3.7	2.1	2.4	2.7	3.1	3.3	3.5	3.6	3.2
1922	2.9	2.8	3.3	3.0	3.0	3.0	2.8	3.1	3.2	3.1	3.4	2.8
1923	3.4	2.9	2.6	3.2*	3.9	3.9	3.1	3.4	4.0	4.8	4.7	4.4
1924	4.5	4.6	4.1	4.1	4.2	3.8	4.6	4.4	5.1	5.9	6.4	5.3
1925	4.6	4.8	4.8	4.0	4.1	4.1	4.6	4.5	4.5	5.3	5.1	4.5
1926	4.1	4.3	4.2	3.9	3.0	4.0	4.6	4.0	4.3	4.5	4.9	4.5
1927	4.1	3.8	4.3	3.6	4.3	3.6	4.3	4.4	4.7	5.0	5.4	4.7
1928	4.3	4.5	4.2	3.8	4.0	3.8	4.4	4.8	4.8	5.3	5.6	4.6
1929	4.2	4.0	3.8	5.0	4.6	3.9	4.7	4.5	4.8	5.4	5.7	4.9
1930	4.6	3.7	4.0	3.6	3.8	3.2	4.4	4.0	4.2	4.4	4.8	3.5
1931	3.7	2.8	3.0	2.9	2.8	2.6	2.7	2.6	2.7	3.4	3.4	2.9
1932	2.8	2.8	2.7	2.9	2.6	2.3	2.3	2.6	2.5	2.9	3.2	2.8
1933	2.5	2.3	2.3	1.9	2.2	2.0	2.3	2.3	2.6	2.8	2.9	2.4
1934	2.6	2.6	2.3	2.3	2.4	2.4	2.3	2.4	2.6	2.8	3.0	2.7
1935	2.4	2.1	2.4	2.2	2.5	2.4	2.6	2.5	2.8	3.4	3.8	2.7
1936	2.8	2.5	2.9	2.4	2.7	2.6	3.0	2.8	3.0	3.6	3.8	3.4
1937	3.0	3.1	2.9	3.1	3.1	3.0	3.3	3.0	3.4	3.4	4.0	3.5
1938	3.0	2.8	2.8	2.4	2.8	2.7	2.9	3.0	3.1	3.7	3.8	3.0
1939	3.1	2.5	3.1	2.4	3.2	3.4	3.0	3.3	2.1	2.2	3.6	3.8

* SEE TEXT

TABLE 5.2 : EXPORTS OF U.K. GOODS (F.O.B.) : FOOD,DRINK AND TOBACCO.
SEASONALLY ADJUSTED (£ MILLIONS)

	JAN	FEB	MAR	APR	MAY	JUN	JUL	AUG	SEP	OCT	NOV	DEC
1919	1	1	2	3	4	3	3	3	3	3	4	4
1920	5	4	5	4	4	5	5	4	4	4	4	4
1921	4	3	3	4	2	3	3	3	3	3	3	3
1922	3	3	4	3	3	3	3	3	3	3	3	3
1923	3	3	3	3*	4	4	3	4	4	4	4	4
1924	4	5	4	4	5	4	5	5	5	5	5	5
1925	4	5	5	4	5	5	5	5	4	5	4	4
1926	4	5	4	4	3	5	5	4	4	4	4	4
1927	4	4	5	4	5	4	4	4	5	4	4	4
1928	4	5	4	4	4	4	4	5	5	5	5	4
1929	4	4	4	5	5	5	5	5	5	5	5	5
1930	5	4	4	4	4	4	4	4	4	4	4	3
1931	4	3	3	3	3	3	3	3	3	3	3	3
1932	3	3	3	3	3	3	2	3	2	3	3	3
1933	3	3	2	2	2	2	2	2	3	2	2	2
1934	3	3	2	3	3	3	2	3	3	2	2	3
1935	2	2	3	3	3	3	3	3	3	3	3	3
1936	3	3	3	3	3	3	3	3	3	3	3	3
1937	3	3	3	4	3	3	3	3	3	3	3	3
1938	3	3	3	3	3	3	3	3	3	3	3	3
1939	3	3	3	3	3	4	3	3	2	2	3	4

* SEE TEXT

TABLE 5.3 : EXPORTS OF U.K. GOODS (F.O.B.) : FOOD,DRINK AND TOBACCO.
SEASONALLY ADJUSTED (£ MILLIONS AT CONSTANT 1924 PRICES)

	JAN	FEB	MAR	APR	MAY	JUN	JUL	AUG	SEP	OCT	NOV	DEC
1920	3.0	2.7	2.8	2.5	2.7	2.8	2.9	2.3	2.6	2.4	2.3	2.2
1921	2.4	2.3	2.2	2.8	1.8	2.0	2.3	2.7	2.7	2.8	2.8	2.9
1922	2.7	2.8	3.3	3.0	3.2	3.2	3.0	3.5	3.3	2.8	2.9	2.9
1923	3.4	3.3	3.0	3.7*	4.7	4.6	3.5	4.0	4.1	4.3	4.0	4.4
1924	4.4	4.8	4.3	4.4	4.8	4.3	5.1	4.8	4.9	4.7	5.0	4.8
1925	4.1	4.7	4.9	4.1	4.5	4.5	4.9	5.0	4.5	4.7	4.4	4.4
1926	4.4	4.9	4.8	4.5	3.4	5.0	4.9	4.3	4.5	4.1	4.2	4.5
1927	4.5	4.5	5.1	4.4	5.1	4.5	4.7	4.8	4.8	4.7	4.7	4.8
1928	4.7	5.3	4.8	4.3	4.6	4.7	4.8	5.3	5.2	5.2	5.1	4.8
1929	4.8	4.8	4.4	6.1	5.8	5.2	5.3	5.2	5.3	5.4	5.4	5.5
1930	5.5	4.9	5.3	5.0	5.5	4.9	5.8	5.3	5.5	5.2	5.4	4.7
1931	5.4	4.5	4.8	4.6	4.6	4.5	4.2	4.0	4.0	4.3	3.9	4.0
1932	4.1	4.3	4.1	4.5	4.1	4.1	3.5	4.0	3.7	4.0	4.1	4.0
1933	3.9	4.0	3.9	3.8	3.8	3.4	3.7	3.9	4.0	3.9	3.7	3.7
1934	4.2	4.7	3.9	4.6	4.1	4.1	3.7	3.8	3.8	3.7	3.7	4.1
1935	3.7	3.5	3.8	3.9	3.9	3.9	4.0	4.0	4.1	4.3	4.5	3.9
1936	4.2	4.2	4.5	4.3	4.1	4.1	4.3	4.1	4.0	4.2	4.1	4.4
1937	4.0	4.5	3.8	4.7	4.1	4.1	4.3	4.0	4.1	3.7	4.1	4.3
1938	3.8	4.0	3.7	3.8	3.8	3.8	3.9	4.3	4.3	4.4	4.3	4.2
1939	4.5	4.1	4.8	4.1	4.6	5.1	4.3	5.0	2.6	2.3	3.3	4.0

* SEE TEXT

TABLE 5.4 : EXPORTS OF U.K. GOODS (F.O.B.) : RAW MATERIALS.
(£ MILLIONS)

	JAN	FEB	MAR	APR	MAY	JUN	JUL	AUG	SEP	OCT	NOV	DEC
1919	4.8	5.6	8.0	6.6	9.9	9.7	11.0	8.4	11.0	11.6	11.8	12.9
1920	16.7	13.8	14.5	12.2	13.2	11.4	12.6	10.5	9.5	9.6	9.4	12.3
1921	7.7	5.9	5.8	2.9	1.4	1.1	2.8	7.1	6.8	7.4	7.0	7.4
1922	7.0	6.9	8.5	7.4	8.8	7.7	8.0	8.9	10.1	9.2	10.1	9.5
1923	9.4	9.5	11.6	11.7*	14.0	11.5	10.8	10.2	9.8	11.6	10.6	10.1
1924	9.5	10.0	9.3	9.5	9.7	7.8	8.3	7.8	8.2	8.7	8.4	9.3
1925	8.3	8.2	7.8	7.3	7.5	5.9	6.9	5.5	6.0	6.9	6.6	7.4
1926	6.4	6.6	7.2	6.0	3.2	2.1	2.3	1.9	1.9	2.6	2.7	4.2
1927	6.6	6.2	7.3	6.3	7.4	6.3	5.8	6.0	5.9	6.2	6.6	5.8
1928	5.8	6.0	6.3	5.3	6.2	6.1	5.4	5.6	4.9	6.2	6.1	6.3
1929	6.6	5.6	6.6	6.8	7.8	6.1	6.9	6.0	6.5	7.1	6.9	6.2
1930	6.9	5.8	6.0	5.4	5.8	4.7	5.2	4.4	5.0	5.3	4.7	4.7
1931	3.7	3.8	4.1	4.1	4.0	4.0	3.8	3.4	3.7	4.3	4.1	4.0
1932	3.6	3.5	3.5	4.0	3.6	3.6	3.5	3.4	3.2	3.9	4.1	3.9
1933	3.8	3.4	3.8	3.1	4.2	3.7	3.9	3.8	4.1	4.3	4.3	3.6
1934	3.9	4.0	4.1	3.8	4.3	3.9	3.8	3.6	4.1	4.5	4.3	3.9
1935	4.7	4.2	4.6	4.0	4.7	4.0	4.6	4.1	3.7	4.7	5.1	4.2
1936	4.1	4.1	4.1	3.9	4.5	3.5	4.6	4.0	4.3	4.8	4.6	4.9
1937	5.1	4.9	5.3	5.6	5.5	5.7	6.0	5.3	5.4	5.8	5.3	4.9
1938	4.7	4.2	4.9	4.5	4.9	4.5	4.7	4.5	4.6	5.3	5.4	4.6
1939	4.7	4.3	4.8	4.2	5.4	5.2	5.3	4.4	2.9	3.8	5.0	4.6

* SEE TEXT

TABLE 5.5 : EXPORTS OF U.K. GOODS (F.O.B.) : RAW MATERIALS.
(£ MILLIONS AT CONSTANT 1924 PRICES)

	JAN	FEB	MAR	APR	MAY	JUN	JUL	AUG	SEP	OCT	NOV	DEC
1920	8.6	6.6	6.7	5.6	6.1	5.4	6.1	5.2	4.8	5.2	5.4	7.8
1921	5.3	4.4	4.7	2.4	1.2	0.9	2.5	6.6	6.3	6.9	6.9	7.5
1922	7.2	7.3	9.0	7.9	9.3	8.2	8.6	9.6	11.1	10.1	10.9	10.2
1923	9.9	9.8	11.5	11.4*	13.9	11.6	11.4	10.9	10.5	12.5	11.0	10.2
1924	9.5	9.9	9.1	9.3	9.6	7.8	8.4	7.9	8.4	8.9	8.5	9.3
1925	8.3	8.2	7.8	7.5	8.0	6.3	7.5	6.0	6.7	7.8	7.5	8.4
1926	7.3	7.6	8.4	7.1	3.8	2.4	2.6	2.1	2.1	2.9	3.0	4.9
1927	8.0	7.5	8.8	7.7	9.0	7.7	7.1	7.3	7.2	7.7	8.2	7.2
1928	7.2	7.4	7.8	6.5	7.6	7.4	6.6	6.9	6.2	7.8	7.8	7.9
1929	8.2	7.0	8.1	8.4	9.7	7.6	8.6	7.6	8.2	9.1	9.0	8.1
1930	9.1	7.7	8.2	7.4	8.1	6.6	7.4	6.5	7.5	8.2	7.3	7.5
1931	6.0	6.1	6.6	6.6	6.6	6.7	6.3	6.0	6.5	7.3	6.8	6.6
1932	5.9	5.7	5.8	6.9	6.3	6.4	6.2	5.9	5.4	6.6	7.1	6.7
1933	6.6	5.9	6.7	5.3	7.1	6.1	6.4	6.2	6.7	7.0	6.9	5.8
1934	6.2	6.2	6.5	6.0	6.8	6.2	6.1	5.8	6.6	7.3	6.9	6.3
1935	7.6	6.8	7.5	6.5	7.6	6.3	7.4	6.6	5.9	7.3	7.8	6.[illegible]
1936	6.3	6.3	6.3	5.9	6.9	5.3	7.0	6.0	6.4	7.1	6.7	6.[illegible]
1937	7.0	6.6	6.9	7.2	6.9	7.0	7.5	6.5	6.7	7.3	6.9	6.[illegible]
1938	6.2	5.7	6.7	6.2	6.8	6.3	6.7	6.3	6.5	7.5	7.5	6.[illegible]
1939	6.8	6.2	7.0	6.0	7.7	7.3	7.6	6.2	3.9	4.9	6.0	5.[illegible]

* SEE TEXT

TABLE 5.6 : EXPORTS OF U.K. GOODS (F.O.B.) : MANUFACTURES.
(£ MILLIONS)

	JAN	FEB	MAR	APR	MAY	JUN	JUL	AUG	SEP	OCT	NOV	DEC
1919	40.2	39.2	42.4	48.3	51.0	51.2	51.0	62.8	51.7	62.6	69.8	72.[illegible]
1920	83.1	66.7	83.4	88.7	100.7	99.1	119.0	99.6	102.2	95.7	103.7	78.[illegible]
1921	79.7	58.2	57.0	52.0	38.7	33.7	36.7	39.9	44.0	50.3	51.1	47.[illegible]
1922	51.8	48.0	51.8	44.3	45.1	40.6	48.6	47.1	48.4	47.0	52.0	44.[illegible]
1923	53.1	44.3	45.9	46.9*	52.8	46.5	44.7	45.4	48.9	53.9	49.4	48.[illegible]
1924	48.8	52.7	46.7	48.3	55.4	49.5	57.2	53.1	48.9	52.8	52.0	52.[illegible]
1925	55.0	55.3	55.5	48.2	51.1	47.7	51.6	49.5	48.8	53.8	48.1	51.[illegible]
1926	48.4	50.8	53.5	41.5	39.1	42.2	49.2	42.7	43.2	44.9	44.1	38.[illegible]
1927	43.7	41.6	49.1	41.5	50.3	44.9	44.8	47.7	48.8	48.7	57.2	45.[illegible]
1928	48.3	45.5	53.4	45.0	46.4	48.0	49.2	50.1	45.2	50.8	49.9	46.[illegible]
1929	53.8	44.3	47.0	47.1	53.4	38.4	53.2	50.8	42.2	50.3	48.6	44.[illegible]
1930	44.7	41.2	42.5	36.7	39.8	33.8	39.7	33.1	32.0	35.9	32.7	27.[illegible]
1931	28.7	24.0	25.6	24.3	26.0	21.7	26.5	22.0	22.2	24.0	22.9	22.[illegible]
1932	23.4	22.6	24.2	26.8	23.2	22.9	22.4	21.7	19.8	22.7	22.5	23.[illegible]
1933	22.1	21.4	25.4	20.5	23.5	21.7	22.8	23.9	24.6	26.1	25.7	22.[illegible]
1934	24.2	22.7	25.6	23.2	25.1	24.9	26.0	25.1	26.3	28.5	27.4	25.[illegible]
1935	27.5	26.8	28.0	25.9	27.1	25.5	28.4	27.2	26.7	30.6	29.3	26.[illegible]
1936	26.6	27.6	28.6	26.0	28.2	24.9	31.5	27.5	28.8	32.2	28.9	30[illegible]
1937	29.9	29.7	34.2	33.4	33.3	34.7	37.4	33.4	34.5	36.7	34.7	33[illegible]
1938	32.6	29.7	33.5	29.3	29.5	28.8	29.0	28.0	31.1	32.3	32.5	29[illegible]
1939	30.4	30.4	32.7	27.4	32.7	30.5	31.0	28.5	17.4	18.0	28.0	30[illegible]

* SEE TEXT

TABLE 5.7 : EXPORTS OF U.K. GOODS (F.O.B.) : MANUFACTURES.
(£ MILLIONS AT CONSTANT 1924 PRICES)

	JAN	FEB	MAR	APR	MAY	JUN	JUL	AUG	SEP	OCT	NOV	DEC
1919	27.2	26.3	27.7	31.8	35.9	35.6	34.5	40.3	32.5	37.9	40.6	40.7
1920	46.4	35.7	43.2	45.3	51.4	51.1	61.7	52.4	54.9	53.2	61.0	49.9
1921	53.9	42.8	44.5	41.9	31.7	28.1	31.1	34.7	39.3	46.6	49.6	47.4
1922	52.3	49.0	53.4	45.7	46.5	41.9	49.6	49.6	52.6	51.1	55.9	48.3
1923	55.9	46.6	47.3	48.4*	54.4	48.4	46.6	48.3	51.5	57.3	51.5	49.0
1924	49.3	52.2	46.7	48.3	56.0	50.5	57.8	53.1	48.9	52.3	51.5	51.9
1925	53.4	54.2	55.0	49.2	53.2	50.2	53.7	52.1	52.5	58.5	52.9	56.9
1926	53.8	57.1	61.5	47.7	44.4	48.0	54.7	47.4	47.5	49.3	49.0	43.9
1927	50.2	48.4	57.8	48.8	59.2	52.2	52.7	56.1	57.4	58.0	68.1	54.5
1928	56.8	54.2	62.8	52.3	53.3	55.2	57.9	59.6	54.5	62.0	60.9	56.4
1929	64.8	53.4	55.3	56.1	65.1	46.8	64.1	62.0	51.5	62.1	60.7	56.5
1930	56.6	53.5	56.7	48.9	53.8	46.3	55.1	46.6	46.4	53.6	48.8	42.5
1931	44.8	37.5	40.0	38.0	41.3	34.4	42.7	36.7	37.0	38.7	36.3	36.0
1932	37.1	35.9	38.4	43.2	38.0	38.8	38.0	36.2	32.5	37.8	37.5	38.7
1933	36.8	36.3	43.1	34.7	39.2	35.6	37.4	39.2	39.7	42.8	41.5	36.5
1934	38.4	35.5	40.0	36.2	39.8	39.5	41.3	39.2	41.7	45.2	43.5	41.0
1935	43.7	42.5	44.4	41.1	42.3	39.8	45.1	43.2	41.7	47.1	44.4	39.7
1936	40.9	41.8	43.3	38.8	42.7	37.2	47.0	40.4	41.7	46.0	40.7	42.1
1937	41.0	39.6	43.8	42.3	41.6	43.4	46.7	41.7	43.1	46.5	44.5	43.2
1938	42.3	39.1	44.7	39.1	39.9	39.5	40.3	39.4	44.4	45.5	45.8	41.4
1939	44.1	43.4	46.7	39.1	46.1	43.0	43.7	40.7	22.9	22.8	33.3	35.2

* SEE TEXT

TABLE 5.8 : EXPORTS OF U.K. GOODS (F.O.B.) : TOTAL.
(£ MILLIONS)

	JAN	FEB	MAR	APR	MAY	JUN	JUL	AUG	SEP	OCT	NOV	DEC
1919	47.3	46.9	53.1	58.5	64.3	64.6	65.3	74.8	66.5	79.1	87.1	90.9
1920	105.9	86.0	103.7	106.3	119.3	116.4	137.5	114.9	117.5	112.3	119.4	96.6
1921	92.8	68.2	66.8	59.9	43.1	38.2	43.2	51.3	55.2	62.3	62.9	59.4
1922	63.1	58.3	64.6	55.6	58.0	52.1	60.4	60.0	62.5	60.4	66.5	58.9
1923	66.9	57.5	60.9	62.9*	71.6	62.9	59.5	60.1	63.8	71.3	65.8	64.1
1924	64.2	68.0	61.1	62.9	70.3	62.0	71.3	66.3	63.3	68.6	68.2	69.3
1925	69.1	69.3	70.3	60.9	64.2	58.9	64.8	61.0	60.7	67.1	61.0	65.8
1926	60.4	62.8	66.4	52.7	45.8	50.1	57.3	49.8	50.7	53.2	53.1	49.7
1927	55.4	52.9	62.1	52.6	63.3	56.0	56.1	59.4	60.6	61.2	70.6	58.8
1928	59.7	57.2	65.0	55.3	58.6	59.5	60.9	62.2	56.6	64.3	63.8	60.4
1929	66.9	55.7	58.6	60.2	67.4	49.9	66.5	63.0	55.1	64.6	63.1	58.4
1930	58.3	51.9	53.9	46.9	51.0	42.8	50.7	42.8	42.7	46.9	44.1	38.5
1931	37.6	31.8	34.0	32.5	33.9	29.4	34.3	29.1	29.8	32.8	31.9	32.1
1932	31.1	30.0	31.2	34.8	30.2	29.7	29.3	28.6	26.2	30.4	31.1	32.4
1933	29.2	27.9	32.6	26.4	30.8	28.5	29.8	31.0	32.2	34.1	34.4	30.4
1934	31.6	30.1	33.1	30.1	32.8	32.1	33.2	32.1	34.0	36.7	36.1	34.3
1935	35.5	34.1	36.0	33.0	35.2	32.9	36.4	34.9	34.1	39.9	39.4	34.9
1936	34.5	35.1	36.5	33.4	36.4	32.1	40.1	35.3	37.0	41.8	38.4	40.5
1937	39.1	38.6	43.5	43.0	42.7	44.4	47.6	42.5	44.3	47.2	45.2	43.9
1938	41.2	37.5	42.2	37.3	38.2	36.9	37.5	36.3	39.8	42.6	42.9	39.1
1939	39.5	38.1	41.6	35.1	42.3	39.9	40.4	37.1	23.1	23.6	37.4	40.2

* SEE TEXT

TABLE 5.9 : EXPORTS OF U.K. GOODS (F.O.B.) : TOTAL.
(£ MILLIONS AT CONSTANT 1924 PRICES)

	JAN	FEB	MAR	APR	MAY	JUN	JUL	AUG	SEP	OCT	NOV	DEC
1919	32.0	31.5	34.7	38.5	45.3	44.9	44.1	47.9	41.8	47.9	50.6	51.4
1920	59.2	46.0	53.7	54.2	60.9	60.0	71.2	60.5	63.2	62.4	70.2	61.1
1921	62.7	50.1	52.2	48.3	35.3	31.8	36.6	44.6	49.3	57.7	61.1	59.4
1922	63.7	59.5	66.6	57.3	59.8	53.7	61.6	63.2	67.9	65.7	71.5	63.3
1923	70.4	60.5	62.8	64.8*	73.8	65.5	62.0	63.9	67.2	75.9	68.5	65.4
1924	64.8	67.3	61.1	62.9	71.0	63.3	72.0	66.3	63.3	67.9	67.5	67.9
1925	67.1	67.9	69.6	62.1	66.9	62.0	67.5	64.2	65.3	72.9	67.0	72.3
1926	67.1	70.6	76.3	60.6	52.0	56.9	63.7	55.3	55.7	58.5	59.0	56.5
1927	63.7	61.5	73.1	61.9	74.5	65.1	66.0	69.9	71.3	72.9	84.0	70.0
1928	70.2	68.1	76.5	64.3	67.4	68.4	71.6	74.0	68.2	78.4	77.8	72.8
1929	80.6	67.1	68.9	71.7	82.2	60.9	80.1	76.8	67.2	79.8	78.9	73.9
1930	73.8	67.4	71.9	62.5	68.9	58.6	70.4	60.3	61.9	70.0	65.8	59.2
1931	58.7	49.7	53.1	50.8	53.8	46.7	55.3	48.5	49.7	52.9	50.6	51.0
1932	49.4	47.6	49.5	56.1	49.5	50.3	49.7	47.7	43.0	50.7	51.8	53.1
1933	48.7	47.3	55.3	44.7	51.3	46.7	48.9	50.8	51.9	55.9	55.5	49.0
1934	50.2	47.0	51.7	47.0	52.1	51.0	52.7	50.2	54.0	58.3	57.3	54.4
1935	56.3	54.1	57.1	52.4	55.0	51.4	57.8	55.4	53.3	61.4	59.7	52.9
1936	53.1	53.2	55.3	49.9	55.2	47.9	59.9	51.9	53.6	59.7	54.1	56.2
1937	53.6	51.5	55.8	54.4	53.4	55.5	59.5	53.1	55.4	59.7	57.9	57.0
1938	53.5	49.3	56.3	49.7	51.6	50.5	52.1	51.1	56.9	60.0	60.4	55.1
1939	57.2	54.4	59.4	50.1	59.6	56.2	56.9	53.0	30.4	29.9	44.5	46.2

* SEE TEXT

TABLE 5.10 : U.K. IMPORTS (C.I.F.) : FOOD, DRINK AND TOBACCO.
(£ MILLIONS)

	JAN	FEB	MAR	APR	MAY	JUN	JUL	AUG	SEP	OCT	NOV	DEC
1919	55.3	45.4	48.6	53.7	63.4	59.6	73.2	70.8	62.9	66.0	62.3	65.8
1920	73.2	57.6	61.7	57.4	65.1	67.3	69.4	61.9	67.3	68.9	61.5	59.3
1921	49.1	47.8	50.9	52.9	50.1	51.9	41.8	50.6	48.2	44.5	41.2	39.1
1922	34.0	32.3	45.3	40.1	43.0	39.9	38.8	37.7	35.4	38.5	45.5	42.[illegible]
1923	47.4	37.1	40.7	41.8*	43.6	44.1	35.2	44.1	38.2	44.8	46.8	47.[illegible]
1924	40.7	42.3	47.5	40.0	52.3	40.5	47.5	46.9	45.9	56.7	56.7	56.[illegible]
1925	51.0	45.2	47.4	48.2	42.6	45.4	46.3	41.3	46.4	49.5	51.0	58.[illegible]
1926	52.4	40.3	45.6	42.2	36.4	43.9	43.5	43.0	44.9	46.9	45.4	46.[illegible]
1927	44.2	38.2	46.9	41.3	41.9	46.9	41.1	42.6	48.0	48.7	52.1	48.[illegible]
1928	43.4	41.7	47.0	41.0	42.7	45.8	43.8	44.6	40.3	48.2	48.4	45.[illegible]
1929	49.6	40.0	42.1	42.6	44.2	39.6	42.2	45.7	45.1	51.2	48.5	46.[illegible]
1930	42.9	37.3	40.0	36.7	39.6	37.7	39.2	37.2	36.7	44.1	40.6	44.[illegible]
1931	36.2	30.0	32.5	32.5	33.3	33.4	35.1	31.8	33.6	40.8	38.6	39.[illegible]
1932	31.3	33.6	31.0	27.6	30.2	31.9	29.3	28.2	30.6	35.0	34.3	32.[illegible]
1933	27.2	25.2	29.2	26.4	30.0	27.3	26.3	27.0	29.8	32.3	32.0	30.[illegible]
1934	29.0	25.6	28.6	25.5	29.7	29.4	26.8	27.4	29.2	35.5	32.5	30[illegible]
1935	27.5	26.4	28.6	27.2	30.1	27.5	29.0	27.0	29.6	37.5	34.4	34[illegible]
1936	31.3	27.5	30.2	28.4	31.6	31.5	29.9	29.0	32.9	38.9	37.1	37[illegible]
1937	32.0	30.7	35.3	32.9	34.2	35.8	34.0	34.8	36.2	43.4	43.1	42[illegible]
1938	36.1	33.2	37.1	32.1	35.2	38.4	36.3	35.1	37.7	39.3	39.1	35[illegible]
1939	35.0	30.2	35.7	30.3	33.6	36.1	32.9	34.6	23.0	29.8	38.6	42[illegible]

* SEE TEXT

TABLE 5.11 : U.K. IMPORTS (C.I.F.) : FOOD, DRINK AND TOBACCO.
SEASONALLY ADJUSTED (£ MILLIONS)

	JAN	FEB	MAR	APR	MAY	JUN	JUL	AUG	SEP	OCT	NOV	DEC
1919	56	51	48	56	62	60	74	71	65	62	58	61
1920	75	65	61	60	64	68	71	62	69	65	58	55
1921	50	54	51	55	49	52	42	50	50	42	39	36
1922	35	36	45	42	42	40	39	38	36	36	43	39
1923	48	42	40	43*	43	44	36	44	39	42	44	44
1924	42	48	47	41	51	41	48	47	47	53	53	52
1925	52	51	47	50	42	46	47	41	48	47	48	54
1926	51	45	46	46	39	45	45	44	45	41	41	42
1927	43	42	48	45	45	48	42	44	48	43	47	44
1928	42	46	48	45	46	47	45	46	40	42	43	41
1929	48	44	43	47	47	40	43	47	45	45	44	42
1930	42	41	41	40	42	38	40	38	37	39	36	40
1931	35	33	33	35	36	34	36	33	34	36	35	36
1932	31	37	32	30	32	33	30	29	31	31	31	29
1933	28	29	29	30	30	27	28	29	29	27	28	28
1934	30	29	29	29	29	29	28	29	29	30	29	28
1935	28	30	29	30	30	27	31	29	29	32	30	32
1936	32	32	30	32	31	31	31	31	32	33	33	35
1937	33	35	35	37	34	36	36	37	36	37	38	39
1938	37	38	37	36	35	38	38	37	37	33	35	33
1939	36	35	36	34	33	36	35	37	23	25	34	39

* SEE TEXT

TABLE 5.12 : U.K. IMPORTS (C.I.F.) : FOOD, DRINK AND TOBACCO.
SEASONALLY ADJUSTED (£ MILLIONS AT CONSTANT 1924 PRICES)

	JAN	FEB	MAR	APR	MAY	JUN	JUL	AUG	SEP	OCT	NOV	DEC
1920	49.3	42.2	37.7	35.5	38.6	40.5	42.5	37.6	42.1	38.7	34.9	34.2
1921	32.7	38.3	36.7	40.1	37.4	40.3	33.3	39.7	42.0	38.5	37.1	35.0
1922	34.7	34.3	42.9	40.0	40.4	39.2	38.6	39.6	38.7	38.7	45.3	41.9
1923	51.1	45.7	43.5	47.3*	47.3	47.3	38.7	47.8	41.1	44.2	46.8	46.3
1924	42.9	47.5	47.5	42.3	52.6	42.7	50.0	47.5	46.1	50.0	50.5	49.5
1925	48.6	48.1	44.8	48.5	41.6	45.5	47.5	41.8	49.5	49.5	50.0	55.7
1926	54.3	48.4	50.0	49.5	40.6	47.9	48.4	47.3	48.4	43.6	44.1	45.2
1927	46.7	45.7	53.9	50.6	48.9	51.6	45.7	47.8	51.6	47.3	51.6	48.4
1928	45.7	50.5	52.2	46.9	48.4	50.0	48.9	50.5	44.9	47.2	48.3	46.1
1929	54.5	48.9	47.3	52.8	54.7	46.5	48.3	54.0	51.7	51.7	51.8	50.0
1930	50.6	50.6	51.9	51.3	55.3	50.0	52.6	50.0	49.3	53.4	50.0	57.1
1931	51.5	49.3	49.3	51.5	52.9	50.7	55.4	50.8	52.3	53.7	50.7	52.9
1932	44.9	53.6	45.7	43.5	46.4	50.0	46.2	44.6	47.7	49.2	49.2	44.6
1933	43.7	46.0	46.8	49.2	49.2	43.5	45.2	46.8	46.0	43.5	45.2	45.2
1934	48.4	46.8	47.5	47.5	47.5	46.0	44.4	43.9	44.6	46.9	45.3	43.7
1935	43.1	45.5	44.6	45.5	45.5	40.3	47.7	44.6	43.9	47.8	44.8	47.8
1936	47.8	47.8	44.8	47.8	45.6	44.9	44.9	43.7	44.4	44.6	45.2	46.7
1937	44.0	46.7	44.9	46.8	43.6	46.2	45.6	47.4	46.2	46.8	48.1	49.4
1938	46.8	48.7	47.4	46.8	45.5	50.0	50.7	51.4	53.6	47.1	50.7	47.8
1939	52.2	50.7	52.2	48.6	46.5	50.7	50.0	54.4	30.3	30.5	39.5	43.8

* SEE TEXT

TABLE 5.13 : U.K. IMPORTS (C.I.F.) : RAW MATERIALS.
(£MILLIONS)

	JAN	FEB	MAR	APR	MAY	JUN	JUL	AUG	SEP	OCT	NOV	DEC
1919	48.5	38.7	33.6	40.0	49.1	43.9	54.3	54.9	57.1	57.1	57.4	72.8
1920	78.1	79.6	76.5	71.6	60.5	57.9	51.9	51.3	44.6	44.3	46.6	48.6
1921	37.0	25.5	17.7	16.5	16.7	18.4	20.2	19.6	20.5	21.3	29.9	27.8
1922	24.6	20.2	22.1	21.4	25.4	25.2	24.2	24.1	21.8	26.4	30.2	32.5
1923	30.3	26.7	27.7	22.9*	23.7	23.7	21.0	22.3	23.6	30.9	32.1	40.0
1924	39.2	32.5	32.1	23.5	38.9	25.8	31.7	28.6	27.3	37.2	36.2	47.5
1925	50.9	38.5	36.6	33.7	31.3	28.8	27.6	27.7	28.3	33.7	39.1	49.0
1926	40.9	32.2	31.9	32.9	24.6	27.6	30.8	30.8	30.0	34.8	38.7	37.4
1927	39.5	29.5	35.2	30.7	28.2	27.0	26.6	22.3	26.4	28.4	28.2	30.0
1928	31.1	31.1	34.0	28.5	29.9	26.5	24.0	24.3	20.6	24.2	30.0	30.9
1929	39.1	27.0	28.5	30.9	29.2	24.5	22.9	24.7	24.2	27.3	30.0	31.2
1930	30.1	24.0	24.1	20.7	23.1	20.4	19.1	17.5	16.5	18.1	16.5	20.6
1931	17.9	13.3	15.1	15.5	14.6	14.1	13.6	12.5	11.2	11.9	15.3	18.5
1932	16.9	15.4	16.5	13.4	13.7	13.5	10.8	11.7	11.2	11.9	13.7	15.6
1933	15.1	13.2	14.1	13.0	14.5	14.0	14.9	16.4	14.5	15.0	17.0	18.9
1934	21.3	18.2	18.2	17.1	16.9	16.9	16.6	17.6	15.2	16.9	16.7	18.7
1935	19.8	16.2	16.5	17.0	18.4	15.7	17.0	16.0	15.3	18.0	19.8	23.6
1936	22.4	18.9	19.6	20.0	19.9	19.3	20.1	18.8	19.6	21.5	22.8	26.1
1937	25.7	22.1	25.0	26.0	25.6	27.4	26.3	26.7	26.5	27.9	28.3	27.3
1938	25.7	22.5	24.0	21.5	20.4	19.4	19.2	20.3	18.0	19.0	18.7	19.8
1939	21.5	17.2	19.6	19.5	22.8	22.1	21.5	22.2	13.5	15.9	23.7	23.2

* SEE TEXT

TABLE 5.14 : U.K. IMPORTS (C.I.F.) : RAW MATERIALS
SEASONALLY ADJUSTED (£MILLIONS)

	JAN	FEB	MAR	APR	MAY	JUN	JUL	AUG	SEP	OCT	NOV	DEC
1919	41	39	33	42	50	47	59	60	65	58	53	60
1920	66	81	75	75	62	62	56	56	50	45	43	40
1921	31	26	17	17	17	20	22	21	23	22	28	23
1922	21	21	22	22	26	27	26	26	25	27	28	27
1923	25	27	27	24*	24	25	23	24	27	31	30	33
1924	33	33	31	25	40	28	34	31	31	38	34	39
1925	43	39	36	35	32	31	30	30	32	34	36	41
1926	34	33	31	34	25	30	33	34	34	35	36	31
1927	33	30	34	32	29	29	29	24	30	29	26	25
1928	26	32	33	30	31	28	26	27	23	24	28	26
1929	33	27	28	32	30	26	25	27	27	28	28	26
1930	25	24	24	22	24	22	21	19	19	18	15	17
1931	15	13	15	16	15	15	15	14	13	12	14	15
1932	14	16	16	14	14	14	12	13	13	12	13	13
1933	13	13	14	14	15	15	16	18	16	15	16	16
1934	18	18	18	18	17	18	18	19	17	17	15	15
1935	17	16	16	18	19	17	18	17	17	18	18	20
1936	19	19	19	21	20	21	22	21	22	22	21	2[illegible]
1937	22	22	24	27	26	29	29	29	30	28	26	2[illegible]
1938	22	23	24	23	21	21	21	22	20	19	17	1[illegible]
1939	18	17	19	20	23	24	23	24	15	16	22	1[illegible]

* SEE TEXT

TABLE 5.15 : U.K. IMPORTS (C.I.F.) : RAW MATERIALS
SEASONALLY ADJUSTED (£ MILLIONS AT CONSTANT 1924 PRICES)

	JAN	FEB	MAR	APR	MAY	JUN	JUL	AUG	SEP	OCT	NOV	DEC
1920	34.0	38.6	34.7	34.6	28.6	29.1	27.3	27.7	25.3	24.2	24.9	25.5
1921	21.4	19.4	13.8	14.3	14.4	17.2	19.6	19.4	21.3	20.6	27.5	23.2
1922	21.6	22.1	23.4	23.4	27.4	28.7	28.0	28.0	27.5	29.7	30.1	29.0
1923	26.3	27.8	26.7	23.3*	23.8	25.3	24.2	25.5	29.0	33.3	31.3	33.3
1924	33.0	32.7	30.4	24.5	39.6	28.0	34.3	31.3	31.6	38.8	34.3	39.0
1925	43.0	39.0	36.0	36.1	34.0	33.3	32.6	33.0	35.6	38.2	40.9	46.6
1926	38.6	37.9	36.0	40.0	29.8	34.9	37.5	38.2	37.8	39.3	40.4	36.5
1927	39.8	36.1	41.0	39.0	35.4	35.4	35.4	29.3	36.6	35.8	32.5	30.9
1928	32.1	39.5	40.7	36.6	37.8	34.1	31.7	33.3	29.1	30.4	35.9	32.5
1929	41.2	33.7	34.6	39.5	37.5	32.5	31.3	34.2	34.2	35.9	36.4	33.8
1930	32.9	32.0	32.9	30.1	33.3	31.0	30.0	27.9	28.4	27.7	23.4	27.0
1931	24.2	21.0	24.2	25.8	24.6	25.0	25.0	24.6	22.8	20.3	23.3	24.6
1932	23.0	26.2	26.7	24.1	24.6	25.0	21.4	22.4	22.0	20.3	22.4	22.4
1933	22.4	22.4	24.6	24.1	25.4	24.6	26.2	29.5	26.2	24.6	25.8	25.8
1934	28.6	28.1	28.6	28.6	27.0	28.6	29.0	30.6	27.4	27.4	24.2	24.2
1935	27.4	25.8	26.2	29.0	30.6	27.0	29.0	27.4	27.0	28.1	27.7	30.8
1936	29.2	29.2	29.2	31.8	30.8	31.8	33.3	31.3	32.8	32.4	30.4	31.0
1937	30.1	29.7	31.2	34.6	32.5	35.8	36.2	35.8	37.5	35.4	33.8	30.3
1938	28.9	31.1	32.9	31.5	29.2	29.6	30.0	31.0	28.2	26.8	23.6	22.5
1939	26.1	24.6	27.5	28.6	32.9	33.8	32.9	33.8	20.0	20.5	26.2	21.8

* SEE TEXT

TABLE 5.16 : U.K. IMPORTS (C.I.F.) : MANUFACTURES.
(£ MILLIONS)

	JAN	FEB	MAR	APR	MAY	JUN	JUL	AUG	SEP	OCT	NOV	DEC
1919	29.9	22.3	23.4	18.1	22.6	19.3	25.0	22.5	28.3	30.2	23.6	30.9
1920	31.5	33.0	38.2	38.1	40.6	44.7	41.4	40.0	40.6	36.3	36.0	34.6
1921	30.5	23.4	24.9	20.4	19.3	17.6	18.0	18.2	17.9	18.7	17.9	18.3
1922	17.7	16.6	20.3	19.0	20.2	18.9	18.6	20.3	19.2	19.7	19.6	19.8
1923	21.7	19.5	21.2	21.4*	21.6	21.2	20.3	21.8	20.9	23.7	22.3	21.6
1924	21.0	21.0	23.7	22.3	30.3	21.8	28.2	26.2	27.0	26.0	25.2	27.1
1925	26.4	25.7	28.4	28.0	29.8	36.2	24.3	22.3	22.7	25.1	24.1	26.9
1926	24.1	23.8	29.0	27.1	19.9	25.6	25.6	27.0	26.3	29.0	28.8	28.9
1927	29.6	25.6	30.9	28.4	25.9	25.1	25.3	24.7	26.5	27.6	26.7	26.4
1928	25.6	25.3	29.2	26.8	25.7	26.2	25.5	27.4	25.6	29.1	27.3	24.4
1929	26.8	23.1	27.2	30.2	29.2	26.4	27.4	29.5	28.4	30.2	28.2	27.8
1930	28.0	25.8	28.1	25.6	27.7	24.5	26.0	24.2	24.6	27.7	21.6	23.8
1931	20.4	19.5	22.3	20.9	21.0	20.2	20.7	20.1	22.6	27.2	28.7	18.2
1932	13.3	20.1	13.0	11.8	11.6	11.8	11.4	13.1	12.1	13.5	13.2	12.7
1933	11.5	10.5	12.8	11.4	12.6	12.2	12.0	13.0	13.1	14.2	14.5	13.6
1934	13.9	13.2	14.8	13.5	14.9	14.4	14.3	14.7	13.2	16.0	15.2	13.8
1935	14.2	13.5	15.1	15.5	15.7	14.3	15.5	15.8	15.5	17.5	16.8	15.9
1936	16.0	15.7	17.9	17.9	17.2	16.4	18.2	17.8	19.1	19.8	18.4	19.2
1937	17.6	18.6	22.1	23.6	22.9	24.4	24.6	24.7	24.6	24.4	25.3	23.3
1938	22.5	19.5	23.2	19.7	19.4	18.1	17.7	18.0	18.7	20.2	19.7	17.8
1939	18.4	17.6	21.9	19.7	21.5	23.3	23.5	23.6	13.0	15.7	21.2	20.0

* SEE TEXT

TABLE 5.17 : U.K. IMPORTS (C.I.F.) : MANUFACTURES.
(£ MILLIONS AT CONSTANT 1924 PRICES)

	JAN	FEB	MAR	APR	MAY	JUN	JUL	AUG	SEP	OCT	NOV	DEC
1919	20.2	15.0	15.3	11.9	15.9	13.4	16.9	14.4	17.8	18.3	13.7	17.5
1920	17.6	17.6	19.8	19.4	20.7	23.0	21.5	21.1	21.8	20.2	21.2	21.9
1921	20.6	17.2	19.5	16.5	15.8	14.7	15.3	15.8	16.0	17.3	17.4	18.3
1922	17.9	16.9	20.9	19.6	20.8	19.5	19.0	21.4	20.9	21.4	21.1	21.3
1923	22.8	20.5	21.9	22.1*	22.3	22.1	21.1	23.2	22.0	25.2	23.2	22.0
1924	21.2	20.8	23.7	22.3	30.6	22.2	28.5	26.2	27.0	25.7	25.0	26.6
1925	25.6	25.2	28.1	28.6	31.0	38.1	25.3	23.5	24.4	27.3	26.5	29.6
1926	26.8	26.7	33.3	31.1	22.6	29.1	28.4	30.0	28.9	31.9	32.0	32.8
1927	34.0	29.8	36.4	33.4	30.5	29.2	29.8	29.1	31.2	32.9	31.8	31.4
1928	30.1	30.1	34.4	31.2	29.5	30.1	30.0	32.6	30.8	35.5	33.3	29.4
1929	32.3	27.8	32.0	36.0	35.6	32.2	33.0	36.0	34.6	37.3	35.2	35.2
1930	35.4	33.5	37.5	34.1	37.4	33.6	36.1	34.1	35.7	41.3	32.2	36.6
1931	31.9	30.5	34.8	32.7	33.3	32.1	33.4	33.5	37.7	43.9	45.6	28.9
1932	21.1	31.9	20.6	19.0	19.0	20.0	19.3	21.8	19.8	22.5	22.0	20.8
1933	19.2	17.8	21.7	19.3	21.0	20.0	19.7	21.3	21.1	23.3	23.4	21.9
1934	22.1	20.6	23.1	21.1	23.7	22.9	22.7	23.0	21.0	25.4	24.1	21.9
1935	22.5	21.4	24.0	24.6	24.5	22.3	24.6	25.1	24.2	26.9	25.5	24.1
1936	24.6	23.8	27.1	26.7	26.1	24.5	27.2	26.2	27.7	28.3	25.9	26.7
1937	24.1	24.8	28.3	29.9	28.6	30.5	30.7	30.9	30.7	30.9	32.4	30.3
1938	29.2	25.7	30.9	26.3	26.2	24.8	24.6	25.4	26.7	28.5	27.7	25.1
1939	26.7	25.1	31.3	28.1	30.3	32.8	33.1	33.7	17.1	19.9	25.2	23.0

* SEE TEXT

TABLE 5.18 : U.K. IMPORTS (C.I.F.) : TOTAL.
(£ MILLIONS)

	JAN	FEB	MAR	APR	MAY	JUN	JUL	AUG	SEP	OCT	NOV	DEC
1919	134.5	106.7	105.8	112.1	135.6	122.9	153.1	148.7	148.6	153.5	143.5	169.6
1920	183.3	170.4	176.6	167.1	166.4	170.3	163.1	153.3	152.8	149.6	144.2	142.7
1921	117.0	97.0	93.8	90.0	86.3	88.2	80.5	88.6	86.9	84.7	89.3	85.3
1922	76.5	69.4	87.9	80.6	88.7	84.3	81.7	82.6	76.8	84.9	95.6	94.9
1923	99.7	83.9	90.0	86.4*	89.5	89.3	76.8	88.7	83.3	99.9	101.6	109.2
1924	101.2	96.7	103.7	86.2	122.0	88.6	108.1	102.2	100.9	120.5	118.7	131.6
1925	128.9	110.2	112.9	110.4	104.3	111.0	98.7	91.7	97.9	108.8	114.6	134.3
1926	117.7	96.8	106.9	102.5	81.2	97.5	100.3	101.1	101.7	111.0	113.3	113.3
1927	113.6	93.9	113.5	100.8	96.4	99.3	93.4	90.1	101.4	105.0	107.4	105.4
1928	100.4	98.8	110.5	96.8	99.4	99.4	95.5	97.7	87.7	102.6	106.9	101.5
1929	116.5	90.9	98.6	104.1	103.4	91.5	93.6	101.0	98.4	110.3	108.2	106.4
1930	101.9	88.2	93.4	83.9	91.0	83.4	85.2	79.9	78.7	90.9	79.4	89.6
1931	75.5	63.7	70.6	70.0	69.6	68.6	70.2	65.3	68.3	80.7	83.2	77.0
1932	62.1	70.2	61.2	53.6	56.0	57.9	51.9	53.3	54.3	60.8	61.5	60.6
1933	54.1	49.1	56.3	51.2	57.3	53.8	53.7	56.8	57.8	61.8	63.7	63.2
1934	64.6	57.4	61.9	56.3	61.8	61.2	58.0	60.0	57.9	68.8	64.6	63.2
1935	61.9	56.4	60.5	59.9	64.5	57.8	61.8	59.1	60.8	73.4	71.5	74.4
1936	70.0	62.3	68.1	66.7	69.2	67.6	68.7	66.1	71.9	80.5	78.7	83.7
1937	75.7	71.7	82.9	83.0	83.2	88.2	85.5	86.6	87.8	96.2	97.3	94.[illegible]
1938	84.9	75.7	84.9	73.7	75.4	76.5	73.9	74.1	75.0	79.0	78.0	74.1
1939	75.6	65.5	78.0	70.1	78.5	82.2	78.3	81.1	49.9	61.8	84.0	86.[illegible]

* SEE TEXT

TABLE 5.19 : U.K. IMPORTS (C.I.F.) : TOTAL.
SEASONALLY ADJUSTED (£ MILLIONS)

	JAN	FEB	MAR	APR	MAY	JUN	JUL	AUG	SEP	OCT	NOV	DEC
1919	128	114	105	119	134	127	161	155	157	148	135	148
1920	174	182	175	177	165	176	171	160	162	145	136	124
1921	111	103	93	95	86	91	84	92	92	82	84	74
1922	73	74	87	85	88	87	86	86	81	82	90	83
1923	95	89	89	92*	89	92	81	92	88	97	96	95
1924	96	103	103	91	121	91	113	106	107	116	112	115
1925	122	118	112	117	103	115	103	96	104	105	108	117
1926	112	103	105	107	86	102	106	106	105	102	103	104
1927	108	100	111	105	102	104	98	95	105	96	98	96
1928	95	105	108	101	105	104	101	103	91	94	98	93
1929	110	97	97	109	109	96	99	106	102	101	99	97
1930	97	94	92	88	96	87	90	84	82	83	72	82
1931	72	68	69	73	74	72	74	69	71	74	76	70
1932	59	75	60	56	59	61	55	56	56	56	56	55
1933	53	55	55	54	57	54	56	59	59	57	59	59
1934	64	64	61	60	61	62	60	62	59	63	60	59
1935	61	63	59	64	64	58	64	61	62	67	67	70
1936	69	70	67	71	68	68	71	69	73	74	73	78
1937	75	80	81	88	82	89	89	90	90	88	91	88
1938	84	85	83	78	74	77	77	77	77	72	73	69
1939	75	73	77	74	77	83	81	84	51	57	78	81

* SEE TEXT

TABLE 5.20 : U.K. IMPORTS (C.I.F.) : TOTAL.
SEASONALLY ADJUSTED (£ MILLIONS AT CONSTANT 1924 PRICES)

	JAN	FEB	MAR	APR	MAY	JUN	JUL	AUG	SEP	OCT	NOV	DEC
1919	86.5	76.5	68.6	78.3	94.4	88.2	108.8	99.4	98.7	89.7	78.5	83.6
1920	97.2	97.3	90.7	90.3	84.2	90.7	88.6	84.2	87.1	80.6	80.0	78.5
1921	75.0	75.7	72.7	76.6	70.5	75.8	71.2	80.0	82.1	75.9	81.6	74.0
1922	73.7	75.5	89.7	87.6	90.7	89.7	87.8	90.5	88.0	89.1	96.8	89.2
1923	100.0	93.7	91.8	94.8*	91.8	95.8	84.4	97.9	92.6	103.2	100.0	96.9
1924	97.0	102.0	103.0	91.0	122.2	92.9	114.1	106.0	107.0	114.9	110.9	112.7
1925	118.4	115.7	110.9	119.4	107.3	121.1	107.3	101.1	111.8	114.1	118.7	128.6
1926	124.4	115.7	120.7	123.0	97.7	115.9	117.8	117.8	115.4	112.1	114.4	118.2
1927	124.1	116.3	130.6	123.5	120.0	120.9	115.3	111.8	123.5	114.3	116.7	114.3
1928	111.8	125.0	127.1	117.4	120.7	119.5	118.8	122.6	109.6	114.6	119.5	112.0
1929	132.5	116.9	114.1	129.8	132.9	117.1	119.3	129.3	124.4	124.7	123.8	122.8
1930	122.8	122.1	122.7	117.3	129.7	119.2	125.0	118.3	118.8	123.9	107.5	126.2
1931	112.5	106.2	107.8	114.1	117.5	114.3	119.4	115.0	118.3	119.4	120.6	111.1
1932	93.7	119.0	95.2	90.3	96.7	103.4	93.2	93.3	91.8	93.3	93.3	90.2
1933	88.3	93.2	93.2	91.5	95.0	88.5	91.8	96.7	95.2	93.4	95.2	95.2
1934	101.6	100.0	95.3	93.8	96.8	98.4	95.2	96.9	93.7	100.0	95.2	93.7
.935	96.8	100.0	93.7	101.6	100.0	90.6	101.6	96.8	96.9	103.1	101.5	106.1
.936	106.2	106.1	101.5	106.0	103.0	101.5	106.0	101.5	105.8	105.7	102.8	108.3
.937	102.7	106.7	103.8	111.4	102.5	111.2	111.2	112.5	112.5	111.4	116.7	114.3
938	109.1	111.8	110.7	104.0	100.0	105.5	106.9	108.5	110.0	101.4	102.8	97.2
939	108.7	104.3	110.0	105.7	108.5	116.9	114.1	120.0	67.1	72.2	92.9	93.1

SEE TEXT

TABLE 5.21 : ECONOMIST SHIPPING FREIGHT INDEX (1913 AVERAGE = 100)

	JAN	FEB	MAR	APR	MAY	JUN	JUL	AUG	SEP	OCT	NOV	DEC
1920	545.4	593.9	588.2	519.4	480.6	463.2	384.4	351.0	360.3	394.8	340.4	240.8
1921	194.6	164.5	162.2	147.5	158.4	165.7	169.9	170.6	154.5	141.8	136.5	134.7
1922	131.6	135.8	135.5	129.5	125.1	117.5	114.5	113.2	110.4	114.4	119.4	117.4
1923	114.0	112.7	115.2	115.5	114.5	106.8	103.4	100.2	103.0	107.9	111.2	111.8
1924	117.1	123.8	122.1	117.2	114.3	108.6	103.7	104.4	110.5	115.5	112.8	111.2
1925	114.5	116.0	106.6	104.2	98.2	91.7	94.9	95.9	98.2	99.5	102.2	104.7
1926	100.6	94.8	89.5	88.0	82.7	89.8	99.7	105.5	112.8	158.0	169.1	126.6
1927	118.6	120.5	118.6	111.1	111.4	106.5	101.6	105.5	107.5	105.8	106.3	102.3
1928	98.5	94.3	93.2	94.6	93.8	91.3	93.7	98.2	99.5	103.9	110.9	113.2
1929	109.6	106.7	102.6	99.1	97.3	92.1	94.8	96.1	95.3	93.3	88.3	86.2
1930	81.2	76.5	75.5	77.1	76.1	75.7	78.1	82.6	83.6	81.7	79.3	81.5
1931	81.2	81.9	81.3	80.8	81.8	78.1	75.0	74.4	74.7	81.7	82.3	82.0
1932	79.2	78.2	78.4	78.8	75.6	71.6	68.9	70.3	74.4	75.1	76.3	78.3
1933	78.9	74.2	71.7	70.7	70.4	70.4	72.5	70.0	72.1	72.3	73.5	75.5
1934	75.2	73.3	71.9	71.6	71.7	72.0	73.3	77.0	77.3	75.2	74.1	74.3
1935	72.0	70.0	70.5	71.6	71.9	72.2	71.3	70.6	74.4	83.5	82.2	82.3
1936	80.4	77.9	77.2	77.3	76.3	77.8	79.4	83.8	86.2	91.1	96.6	110.6
1937	116.5	115.5	118.5	129.1	133.1	134.9	132.8	139.0	145.0	140.7	125.6	108.6
1938	107.9	102.1	99.2	97.7	97.8	96.1	95.2	95.7	97.2	95.6	94.1	92.8
1939	92.8	93.1	91.0	91.8	95.6	92.0	90.4	91.6				

TABLE 5.22 : ECONOMIST SHIPPING FREIGHT INDEX.
SEASONALLY ADJUSTED (1913 AVERAGE = 100)

	JAN	FEB	MAR	APR	MAY	JUN	JUL	AUG	SEP	OCT	NOV	DEC
1920	540	598	599	531	493	481	399	357	357	373	321	234
1921	193	166	165	151	162	172	176	174	153	134	129	131
1922	130	137	138	132	128	122	119	115	109	108	113	114
1923	113	114	117	118	117	111	107	102	102	102	105	109
1924	116	125	124	120	117	113	108	106	110	109	106	108
1925	113	117	109	107	101	95	98	98	97	94	96	102
1926	100	96	91	90	85	93	103	107	112	149	160	123
1927	117	121	121	114	114	111	105	107	107	100	100	99
1928	97	95	95	97	96	95	97	100	99	98	105	110
1929	108	108	104	101	100	96	98	98	95	88	83	84
1930	80	77	77	79	78	79	81	84	83	77	75	79
1931	80	83	83	83	84	81	78	76	74	77	78	80
1932	78	79	80	81	78	74	71	72	74	71	72	76
1933	78	75	73	72	72	73	75	71	72	68	69	73
1934	74	74	73	73	74	75	76	78	77	71	70	72
1935	71	71	72	73	74	75	74	72	74	79	78	80
1936	80	78	79	79	78	81	82	85	85	86	91	108
1937	115	116	121	132	137	140	138	141	144	133	119	106
1938	107	103	101	100	100	100	99	97	96	90	89	90
1939	92	94	93	94	98	96	94	93				

TABLE 5.23 : TONNAGE OF SHIPS (WITH CARGOES) LEAVING BRITAIN.
(TENS OF THOUSANDS OF TONS)

	JAN	FEB	MAR	APR	MAY	JUN	JUL	AUG	SEP	OCT	NOV	DEC
1919	230	237	274	267	332	285	293	264	306	313	311	333
1920	325	310	318	270	293	310	338	297	302	267	315	328
1921	262	262	294	189	165	198	281	378	410	406	394	400
1922	392	389	481	419	510	496	483	585	573	559	565	515
1923	528	499	604	598	627	634	554	605	608	653	606	551
1924	510	487	510	529	588	529	579	563	569	586	550	517
1925	536	476	509	498	542	508	564	481	523	573	512	508
1926	514	480	528	522	234	335	355	334	341	336	301	418
1927	495	462	538	519	552	538	561	565	572	529	529	492
1928	493	475	538	486	550	570	549	597	547	572	549	516
1929	541	462	551	551	601	575	618	648	597	622	586	517
1930	579	495	534	526	598	534	571	589	579	581	511	489
1931	469	423	466	465	504	507	536	502	502	538	460	460
1932	467	422	439	461	442	483	501	468	500	456	457	447
1933	439	409	443	420	479	485	482	511	516	476	478	426
1934	449	414	455	425	476	490	484	524	493	492	468	438
1935	465	398	462	442	503	472	520	531	488	515	494	439
1936	453	410	427	435	493	473	522	511	504	523	464	466
1937	453	428	472	514	509	545	582	549	563	550	491	484
1938	448	415	458	465	480	519	524	538	548	535	489	470
1939	465	414	469	477	541	571	559	552				

TABLE 5.24 : TONNAGE OF SHIPS (WITH CARGOES) LEAVING BRITAIN.
SEASONALLY ADJUSTED (TENS OF THOUSANDS OF TONS)

	JAN	FEB	MAR	APR	MAY	JUN	JUL	AUG	SEP	OCT	NOV	DEC
1919	235	263	275	281	337	286	281	250	290	297	310	341
1920	332	344	319	284	297	311	324	282	286	253	314	335
1921	268	291	295	199	167	199	269	359	388	385	393	409
1922	401	432	483	441	518	497	463	555	542	530	563	527
1923	540	554	606	629	636	636	531	574	576	619	604	564
1924	522	541	512	556	597	530	555	534	539	555	548	529
1925	548	528	511	524	550	509	540	456	495	543	510	520
1926	526	533	530	549	237	336	340	317	323	318	300	427
1927	506	513	540	546	560	539	537	536	541	501	527	503
1928	504	527	540	511	558	571	526	566	518	542	547	528
1929	553	513	553	579	610	576	592	615	565	590	584	529
1930	592	550	536	553	607	535	547	559	548	551	509	500
1931	480	470	468	489	511	508	513	476	475	510	459	470
1932	478	468	440	485	449	484	480	444	473	432	456	457
1933	449	454	444	442	486	486	462	485	488	451	476	436
1934	459	460	456	447	483	491	464	497	467	466	466	448
1935	476	442	464	465	510	473	498	504	462	488	492	449
1936	463	455	428	457	500	474	500	485	477	496	463	477
1937	463	475	474	540	516	546	557	521	533	521	489	495
1938	458	461	460	489	487	520	502	510	519	507	487	481
1939	475	460	471	502	549	572	536	523				

TABLE 5.25 : TONNAGE OF SHIPS (WITH CARGOES) ENTERING BRITAIN.
(TENS OF THOUSANDS OF TONS).

	JAN	FEB	MAR	APR	MAY	JUN	JUL	AUG	SEP	OCT	NOV	DEC
1919	183	181	194	220	237	241	281	279	284	288	268	300
1920	258	242	296	274	304	311	328	363	327	325	311	310
1921	293	254	287	262	308	327	336	342	340	342	313	307
1922	291	258	323	332	410	382	405	399	371	413	377	372
1923	390	310	368	407	433	467	463	453	437	480	429	471
1924	392	346	409	406	488	487	531	511	501	511	457	496
1925	427	382	442	432	452	512	497	482	487	506	475	455
1926	437	381	449	462	391	506	610	694	629	657	624	574
1927	500	409	481	477	533	522	531	576	520	544	500	465
1928	458	416	474	484	528	529	544	535	516	563	480	506
1929	468	391	457	515	538	535	596	588	590	583	513	494
1930	479	427	484	498	579	581	605	564	588	557	496	512
1931	451	401	478	459	511	558	564	568	534	522	498	485
1932	445	483	440	461	507	541	533	544	521	518	462	481
1933	440	403	476	464	524	531	549	565	558	543	498	491
1934	481	425	499	497	530	571	571	573	542	552	517	508
1935	456	422	471	507	555	544	607	593	583	561	524	539
1936	560	470	521	505	559	608	617	646	598	600	563	555
1937	487	482	576	542	600	629	642	672	601	610	614	586
1938	533	484	560	530	603	613	606	642	591	589	537	550
1939	505	454	529	523	615	639	657	662				

TABLE 5.26 : TONNAGE OF SHIPS (WITH CARGOES) ENTERING BRITAIN.
SEASONALLY ADJUSTED (TENS OF THOUSANDS OF TONS).

	JAN	FEB	MAR	APR	MAY	JUN	JUL	AUG	SEP	OCT	NOV	DEC
1919	201	222	208	237	232	227	255	251	267	267	271	304
1920	283	296	318	295	298	293	298	326	308	302	315	314
1921	322	311	308	282	302	308	305	307	320	317	317	311
1922	320	316	347	357	402	360	368	359	349	383	381	377
1923	429	379	395	438	424	440	420	407	411	446	434	477
1924	431	423	439	437	478	459	482	459	471	474	462	502
1925	469	468	475	465	443	483	451	433	458	470	480	461
1926	480	466	482	497	383	477	554	624	592	610	631	581
1927	549	501	516	513	522	492	482	518	489	505	506	471
1928	503	509	509	521	517	499	494	481	485	523	485	513
1929	514	479	491	554	527	505	541	528	555	541	519	500
1930	526	523	520	536	567	548	549	507	553	517	502	519
1931	496	491	513	494	501	526	512	510	502	485	504	491
1932	489	591	472	496	497	510	484	489	490	481	467	487
1933	483	493	511	499	513	501	498	508	525	504	504	497
1934	528	520	536	535	519	539	518	515	510	512	523	515
1935	501	516	506	546	544	513	551	533	548	521	530	546
1936	615	575	559	543	548	573	560	581	562	557	569	562
1937	535	590	618	583	588	593	583	604	565	566	621	594
1938	586	592	601	570	591	578	550	577	556	547	543	557
1939	555	555	568	603	603	596	597	595				

6 Money and Banking

TABLES

adjusted. Monthly, January 1920–December 1939. 101

SOURCES
Table 6.1 *London and Cambridge Economic Service Bulletin*
Tables 6.2–6.9, 6.14–6.15 London clearing banks' monthly statement
Tables 6.10–6.13 January 1919–March 1931: report of the (Macmillan) Committee on Finance and Industry, *British Parliamentary Papers*, 1930–1 (Cmd. 3897), XIII; April 1931–December 1936: *Bank of England Statistical Summary* (*BESS*)
Tables 6.16–6.17 *BESS*
Tables 6.18–6.19 January 1920–December 1924: R. M. Goodwin, 'Studies in money', (unpublished Ph.D. thesis, Harvard, 1941); January 1925–February 1931: Report of the Macmillan Committee *op. cit.*; April 1931–December 1939: *BESS*

The series of bank clearings presented in Table 6.1 is the sum of Metropolitan, Country and Provincial clearings. The Metropolitan and Country clearings were London-based, but a third London clearing, that for 'the Town', was largely dominated by the financial payments of the City of London, particularly the Stock Exchange, and it has not been included here. The series are derived from the returns of the committee of the London clearing bankers and the Provincial clearings, returns which were widely published in the contemporary financial press. Membership of the Provincial clearings varied from one to another and over time, but given the importance of the London clearing bankers' committee it is useful to list its members. Throughout the inter-war period membership covered ten banks: Midland; Barclays; Lloyds; Westminster; National Provincial; Martins; Glyn; Mills; National; Coutts; and Williams Deacons.[1] In addition, from the beginning of 1936, the District Bank was admitted to the committee and this affects all original series related to the London clearing banks as a group. In total these banks accounted for the great bulk of commercial banking business conducted in the country. The London clearings, however, also included the transactions of banks for which committee members acted as agents, as well as some limited Bank of England business.

The London bankers' Metropolitan clearing covered an area within half an hour's journey from the City, but excluded the inner City itself which was covered by the Town clearing. It included cheques, bills and other drafts payable at the bank offices within the area. The Country clearing covered all cheques drawn on the branches of Clearing House members which were outside the Town and Metropolitan areas, as well as those drawn on provincial banks for which clearing banks acted as agents. Its business was restricted to England and Wales, and to business not covered by the Provincial clearings. The Provincial clearings were local arrangements in major provincial centres (eleven in 1927), of which Manchester and Liverpool were prominent (together accounting for about sixty per cent of the total business of the late 1920s and early 1930s). They dealt with cheques and other drafts for which both the receiving and paying banks were members of the local clearing. Used on its own the Provincial clearing series is the most inconsistent because of frequent changes in both the membership within particular local clearings and in the number of Provincial clearings included within the reported figures. It is true, however, that variations of the former sort would be offset within the aggregated clearing figures by opposite movements in the Country clearing – as the business of particular provincial offices moved from one of the clearings to the other. But an element of uncertainty remains as another alternative to Provincial clearing was unreported local clearings. The major changes of this nature were probably the additions to the Provincial clearing figures of two previously unreported local clearings, at Hull (1921) and Bradford (1926). It has been estimated that the total effect of these additions to the total Metropolitan, Country and Provincial clearings was no more than two per cent however.[2] Thus, the aggregated series is largely consistent over time and can be seen as an index measuring 'the flow of total non-financial money payments in the economy'.[3]

The other main collection of monetary series refers to stock, rather than turnover figures. Tables 6.2–6.15 relate to the major asset and liability items on the balance sheets of the London clearing banks. For the period, regular series commence with the publication of monthly returns by the London clearing bankers' committee from early 1921.[4] The biggest break in the original data was caused by the inclusion of the District Bank from 1936, but in the tables presented here the District has been excluded in order to ensure consistency. The main asset items are holdings of currency and balances at the Bank of England; money at call and short notice; bills discounted; advances; and investments. Although the figures are based on averages of the weekly statement of the ten clearing banks it is important to note that not all the balances were struck on the one day, and that this variation of accounting dates produces some distortion when the figures are aggregated. In particular it is thought that the practice of 'window-dressing', which did not cease until the end of 1946, overstated the value of the banks' cash assets, with a corresponding understatement of other asset items. For liabilities the problem of double-counting applies mainly to total deposits. This series appeared in the clearing banks' monthly statement and consisted of liabilities on 'current, deposit and other accounts', which included some inter-bank liabilities such as cheques still in the course of collection, other items in transit and some internal accounts of the banks themselves. Thus, the aggregated figure overstates the extent of the banks' collective liabilities to the general public, and does not correspond to the sum of the two series in Tables 6.10 and 6.12 which were compiled from a different source. In fact the two separate series for current accounts and deposit accounts also differ from total deposits in that they exclude the Irish business of the National Bank. Unfortunately, the two separate deposit series published by the *Bank of England Statistical Summary* (*BESS*) continued in this form only until the close of 1936.[5]

Apart from providing a breakdown of commercial bank deposits the *BESS* also estimated the circulation of currency in the hands of the general public during the period. This series is presented in Tables 6.16 and 6.17. The figures include the notes issued by the Bank of England, the Scottish and Irish banks, plus the estimated coin circulation; minus notes and coin held by the London clearing banks (including the District from January 1936) and the Scottish and Irish banks. From May 1932 gold coin has been excluded from the coin circulation. It is important to be aware that the general series refers to the whole of the United Kingdom, while the London clearing banks series are to all intents and purposes confined to England and Wales.[6] This qualification also applies to bankers' deposits at the Bank of England which appear in Tables 18 and 19, because the figures relate to *all* commercial banks (including the

District Bank) whose businesses were conducted largely in the United Kingdom.

NOTES

1 For convenience, generally-recognised names only have been used.

2 E. H. Phelps-Brown and G. L. S. Shackle, 'An Index of Real Turnover, 1919–36', *Oxford Economic Papers*, I (1938), pp. 33, 37.

3 E. H. Phelps-Brown and G. L. S. Shackle, *Statistics of Monetary Circulation in England and Wales, 1919–37* LCES Special Memorandum 46 (1938), pp. 12f.

4 Although monthly estimates for many of the items from January 1919 appear in the report of the (Macmillan) Committee on Finance and Industry. *BPP*, XIII, pp. 284–9.

5 From 1936 the District is included, and from 1938 the National's Irish business is added. R. M. Goodwin, 'Studies in Money' (unpublished Ph.D. thesis, Harvard, 1941), p. 185, considers a possible means of extending the series to later years.

6 Of its estimate the *BESS* (January 1939, p. 4) also remarked that: 'It is impracticable, in general, to eliminate currency held abroad'.

TABLE 6.1 : BANK CLEARINGS - SUM OF METROPOLITAN, COUNTRY AND PROVINCIAL (£ MILLIONS)

	JAN	FEB	MAR	APR	MAY	JUN	JUL	AUG	SEP	OCT	NOV	DEC
1919	570	498	530	525	601	572	702	610	612	701	712	738
1920	849	786	873	787	778	745	803	714	713	746	694	639
1921	659	563	585	566	499	475	505	494	482	537	507	508
1922	520	480	543	484	543	485	543	498	458	527	507	485
1923	555	486	529	504	526	500	527	477	441	540	498	494
1924	547	503	523	510	545	486	567	483	491	564	523	540
1925	594	510	551	527	548	510	582	495	493	574	528	550
1926	569	502	552	508	464	497	533	456	458	529	521	517
1927	564	493	560	520	557	511	565	512	490	577	551	540
1928	584	532	568	525	570	534	582	512	481	591	546	541
1929	608	517	544	555	547	523	601	514	484	586	550	529
1930	592	502	539	516	542	472	556	458	453	523	481	491
1931	552	450	483	463	462	457	508	425	411	498	444	464
1932	513	449	464	476	444	438	488	432	410	474	458	469
1933	509	444	476	432	492	443	513	448	441	507	486	475
1934	573	471	511	489	499	493	529	466	438	553	507	511
1935	595	493	519	507	536	497	599	505	475	580	544	550
1936	628	556	567	545	574	540	635	529	534	641	598	623
1937	674	592	626	644	597	619	677	568	570	642	621	619

TABLE 6.2 : LONDON CLEARING BANKS ASSETS : COIN, BANK AND CURRENCY NOTES, AND BALANCES WITH THE BANK OF ENGLAND (£ MILLIONS)

	JAN	FEB	MAR	APR	MAY	JUN	JUL	AUG	SEP	OCT	NOV	DEC
1921				205	207	222	212	210	213	221	207	23[illegible]
1922	213	210	207	210	[illegible]	211	204	202	198	200	198	20[illegible]
1923	206	193	191	196	193	198	197	193	195	195	193	20[illegible]
1924	200	193	189	192	191	202	193	192	193	193	193	20[illegible]
1925	200	199	190	193	189	202	198	196	195	193	191	20[illegible]
1926	196	191	190	190	191	202	198	196	194	196	195	20[illegible]
1927	200	195	192	196	195	203	197	195	196	199	196	2[illegible]
1928	201	192	190	191	192	198	197	195	197	196	197	2[illegible]
1929	202	190	188	192	192	196	193	192	195	193	190	2[illegible]
1930	195	185	184	191	190	193	194	191	190	192	192	2[illegible]
1931	198	190	184	178	179	187	184	180	174	176	173	1[illegible]
1932	180	173	174	173	179	191	191	193	193	193	193	2[illegible]
1933	214	208	207	219	206	213	205	208	215	218	216	2[illegible]
1934	223	209	219	222	218	199	210	196	207	213	210	2[illegible]
1935	225	213	214	217	219	217	219	213	208	204	214	2[illegible]
1936	220	221	209	220	213	218	218	227	222	219	225	2[illegible]
1937	231	222	218	222	225	234	227	226	230	226	227	2[illegible]
1938	243	235	237	238	223	239	236	233	226	226	224	2[illegible]
1939	240	235	224	221	228	227	226	224	259	246	236	2[illegible]

TABLE 6.3 : LONDON CLEARING BANKS ASSETS : COIN, BANK AND CURRENCY NOTES, AND BALANCES WITH THE BANK OF ENGLAND. (£ MILLIONS) SEASONALLY ADJUSTED

	JAN	FEB	MAR	APR	MAY	JUN	JUL	AUG	SEP	OCT	NOV	DEC
1921				207	210	220	210	212	215	223	209	220
1922	207	212	211	214	214	209	204	204	200	202	200	200
1923	200	194	195	197	196	196	197	195	197	197	195	198
1924	194	194	193	193	194	200	193	194	195	195	195	200
1925	194	200	194	194	192	200	198	198	197	195	193	195
1926	190	192	194	191	194	200	198	198	196	198	197	198
1927	194	196	196	197	198	201	197	197	198	201	198	198
1928	195	193	194	192	195	196	197	197	199	198	199	198
1929	196	191	192	193	195	194	193	194	197	195	192	197
1930	189	186	188	192	193	191	194	193	192	194	194	199
1931	192	191	188	179	182	185	184	182	176	177	175	176
1932	175	174	178	174	182	189	191	195	195	195	195	198
1933	208	210	211	221	209	211	205	210	217	220	218	204
1934	216	211	224	224	222	197	210	198	209	215	212	207
1935	218	215	219	219	223	215	219	215	210	206	216	212
1936	213	223	213	222	216	216	218	229	224	221	227	226
1937	224	224	223	224	229	231	227	228	232	228	229	227
1938	236	237	242	240	227	236	236	235	228	228	226	225
1939	233	237	229	223	232	224	226	226	261	248	238	253

TABLE 6.4 : LONDON CLEARING BANKS ASSETS ; MONEY AT CALL AND SHORT NOTICE (£ MILLIONS)

	JAN	FEB	MAR	APR	MAY	JUN	JUL	AUG	SEP	OCT	NOV	DEC
1921				100	104	106	113	109	108	111	104	114
1922	123	119	109	114	115	119	116	110	109	110	102	111
1923	113	107	109	114	112	117	108	104	106	105	109	115
1924	104	96	97	101	104	112	102	105	112	107	106	117
1925	116	125	112	116	108	117	118	121	115	116	115	122
1926	118	115	114	121	117	126	123	121	117	120	122	133
1927	129	122	123	128	131	144	138	142	139	147	139	160
1928	150	146	150	156	151	157	150	140	145	148	146	165
1929	150	138	136	145	146	153	145	145	150	150	144	143
1930	144	130	135	136	139	146	145	137	136	145	139	144
1931	144	116	114	117	132	133	131	113	107	114	104	119
1932	117	110	113	112	113	113	123	118	114	117	117	127
1933	114	112	109	105	98	101	96	91	91	89	99	119
1934	130	118	120	132	131	140	138	139	137	136	135	151
1935	137	127	133	137	142	143	145	144	147	141	147	159
1936	154	151	155	154	152	152	151	156	158	155	172	186
1937	170	158	162	169	160	162	155	154	154	156	151	155
1938	145	137	143	142	138	147	151	145	139	141	140	150
1939	134	130	133	137	135	140	146	142	140	154	136	167

TABLE 6.5 : LONDON CLEARING BANKS ASSETS : MONEY AT CALL AND SHORT NOTICE. SEASONALLY ADJUSTED (£ MILLIONS)

	JAN	FEB	MAR	APR	MAY	JUN	JUL	AUG	SEP	OCT	NOV	DEC
1921				100	105	102	112	110	110	112	106	107
1922	120	124	112	114	116	115	115	111	111	111	104	104
1923	110	111	112	114	113	113	107	105	108	106	111	107
1924	102	100	100	101	105	109	101	106	114	108	108	109
1925	114	130	115	116	109	113	117	122	117	117	117	114
1926	115	119	117	121	118	122	121	123	119	121	124	124
1927	126	126	127	129	133	140	136	144	141	148	141	150
1928	146	151	155	157	152	152	148	142	148	149	149	154
1929	146	143	140	146	147	148	143	147	153	151	147	134
1930	141	135	139	136	141	141	144	139	139	147	141	135
1931	141	120	118	117	133	129	129	115	109	116	106	112
1932	115	114	116	113	114	110	122	119	116	118	119	118
1933	111	116	112	105	99	98	95	92	93	90	101	111
1934	127	123	124	132	132	136	136	141	140	137	137	141
1935	134	132	137	137	143	139	143	146	150	142	149	149
1936	150	157	160	154	154	147	149	158	161	157	175	174
1937	166	164	167	169	162	157	153	156	157	158	153	145
1938	142	142	148	142	139	143	149	147	142	142	142	140
1939	131	134	136	137	136	136	144	144	143	156	138	156

TABLE 6.6 : LONDON CLEARING BANKS ASSETS : BILLS DISCOUNTED (£ MILLIONS)

	JAN	FEB	MAR	APR	MAY	JUN	JUL	AUG	SEP	OCT	NOV	DEC
1921				278	308	350	376	383	398	413	434	428
1922	442	404	354	323	330	[illegible]	[illegible]	309	299	312	301	301
1923	323	289	253	252	265	274	279	268	263	278	272	297
1924	295	264	227	227	238	248	262	237	228	241	237	237
1925	248	237	205	194	203	208	231	226	243	247	238	234
1926	234	212	190	190	188	213	236	229	221	227	222	233
1927	246	222	199	197	200	216	219	207	213	234	235	237
1928	260	226	198	250	201	237	259	256	246	250	251	261
1929	277	263	217	194	197	218	236	227	224	229	233	229
1930	245	220	184	210	248	273	286	281	286	298	311	322
1931	330	301	240	211	224	266	281	264	237	238	241	246
1932	239	208	217	240	247	278	317	374	392	391	391	408
1933	431	386	348	338	346	352	362	359	355	343	317	311
1934	284	250	202	212	222	228	224	222	213	216	232	25[illegible]
1935	284	265	207	199	218	244	274	287	299	297	293	32[illegible]
1936	337	288	248	264	304	322	341	338	336	343	322	31[illegible]
1937	340	302	249	239	242	257	279	273	277	292	293	29[illegible]
1938	325	283	235	245	275	286	297	300	284	262	266	24[illegible]
1939	251	207	187	180	195	242	271	272	227	279	242	22[illegible]

TABLE 6.7 : LONDON CLEARING BANKS ASSETS : BILLS DISCOUNTED
SEASONALLY ADJUSTED (£ MILLIONS)

	JAN	FEB	MAR	APR	MAY	JUN	JUL	AUG	SEP	OCT	NOV	DEC
1921				320	340	354	359	371	387	393	415	401
1922	397	405	412	372	363	354	322	299	291	297	288	282
1923	290	290	295	290	293	277	266	259	256	265	260	278
1924	265	265	264	261	263	251	250	229	222	230	227	222
1925	223	238	239	223	224	210	221	219	237	235	228	219
1926	210	213	221	219	208	215	225	222	215	216	213	218
1927	221	223	232	227	221	219	209	200	207	223	225	222
1928	233	227	231	288	222	240	247	248	240	238	240	245
1929	249	264	253	223	218	221	225	220	218	218	223	215
1930	220	221	214	242	274	276	273	272	279	284	298	302
1931	296	302	279	243	247	269	268	255	231	227	231	231
1932	215	209	253	276	273	281	303	362	382	373	374	383
1933	387	387	405	389	382	356	346	347	346	327	304	292
1934	255	251	235	244	245	231	214	215	207	206	222	239
1935	255	266	241	229	241	247	262	278	291	283	281	302
1936	303	289	289	304	336	326	326	327	327	327	308	295
1937	305	303	290	275	267	260	266	264	270	278	281	277
1938	292	284	274	282	304	289	284	290	277	250	255	229
1939	225	208	218	207	215	245	259	263	221	266	232	209

TABLE 6.8 : LONDON CLEARING BANKS ASSETS : INVESTMENTS
(£ MILLIONS)

	JAN	FEB	MAR	APR	MAY	JUN	JUL	AUG	SEP	OCT	NOV	DEC
1921				323	320	325	326	316	322	321	326	335
1922	350	378	386	396	410	406	406	409	401	389	385	379
1923	377	369	353	346	344	350	357	357	355	354	356	357
1924	363	358	353	349	344	341	340	338	332	328	325	321
1925	314	305	299	295	291	284	277	273	271	276	277	277
1926	278	271	263	261	260	259	262	263	264	266	267	266
1927	267	259	255	252	252	252	253	252	249	253	252	249
1928	260	259	251	248	248	247	251	252	259	258	256	260
1929	265	264	259	259	259	259	257	257	256	255	249	250
1930	248	244	240	240	247	248	256	265	270	272	280	285
1931	297	309	311	309	290	288	300	302	304	304	300	297
1932	283	280	282	288	300	340	349	364	383	412	425	472
1933	472	498	510	517	530	544	554	563	563	559	569	565
1934	558	560	547	534	542	549	550	557	563	575	589	594
1935	593	606	614	618	620	624	615	615	618	626	621	605
1936	601	601	605	608	610	612	610	612	620	626	627	631
1937	639	641	637	631	627	624	617	616	611	609	604	605
1938	606	603	604	608	601	600	603	612	616	616	613	606
1939	595	588	582	581	575	571	568	570	573	576	581	580

TABLE 6.9 : LONDON CLEARING BANKS ASSETS : ADVANCES (£ MILLIONS)

	JAN	FEB	MAR	APR	MAY	JUN	JUL	AUG	SEP	OCT	NOV	DEC
1921				870	857	833	831	817	804	805	793	780
1922	770	766	765	763	754	741	739	732	729	741	750	750
1923	744	754	759	762	761	764	765	760	761	763	767	774
1924	778	787	802	807	805	808	808	809	811	824	828	828
1925	835	838	857	864	865	867	868	856	851	854	853	863
1926	874	880	892	890	893	889	890	888	894	901	903	905
1927	903	908	916	918	919	921	925	924	925	923	921	920
1928	938	933	945	949	951	947	948	947	946	954	957	960
1929	972	983	996	1002	992	993	1002	997	988	990	990	989
1930	985	988	991	984	972	977	967	951	942	939	935	929
1931	924	925	936	940	935	923	913	909	911	910	900	900
1932	904	902	902	881	871	852	836	816	802	795	785	773
1933	764	766	766	764	775	775	768	758	750	747	737	736
1934	735	742	753	759	755	757	759	756	754	756	755	754
1935	753	756	767	775	770	775	775	765	763	773	774	779
1936	788	800	824	838	839	847	853	845	850	860	863	858
1937	853	875	905	919	923	934	941	938	943	954	955	948
1938	935	950	964	963	951	949	949	939	939	939	931	935
1939	937	946	958	962	958	957	951	954	978	979	961	968

TABLE 6.10 : LONDON CLEARING BANKS CURRENT ACCOUNTS (£ MILLIONS)

	JAN	FEB	MAR	APR	MAY	JUN	JUL	AUG	SEP	OCT	NOV	DEC
1919	984	931	952	962	971	1113	1012	1009	1032	1041	1063	1121
1920	1135	1114	1112	1119	1075	1104	1080	1077	1074	1089	1073	1114
1921	1100	1045	1003	990	996	1030	1025	1006	1013	1037	1007	1045
1922	1038	1023	988	989	995	1013	1005	979	964	991	984	1011
1923	1016	976	950	959	952	985	973	945	943	952	942	995
1924	975	937	934	940	941	980	955	932	945	944	936	983
1925	956	934	922	906	885	935	917	904	911	920	919	962
1926	934	909	899	895	896	943	931	922	909	929	920	969
1927	937	905	897	904	908	962	938	930	934	954	934	983
1928	967	930	920	931	928	977	969	944	946	958	949	1026
1929	989	948	930	932	918	970	955	927	931	921	903	958
1930	918	876	877	901	897	954	936	916	928	929	925	99[illegible]
1931	962	913	895	886	887	951	935	889	885	859	871	86[illegible]
1932	818	775	799	789	810	868	903	898	907	914	925	99[illegible]
1933	980	955	936	950	962	1006	993	990	984	983	980	101[illegible]
1934	974	931	910	919	925	954	960	939	948	960	975	104[illegible]
1935	1034	1009	994	1004	1015	1072	1084	1068	1080	1064	1080	114[illegible]
1936	1128	1086	1086	1107	1118	1175	1183	1172	1187	1197	1200	124[illegible]

TABLE 6.11 : LONDON CLEARING BANKS CURRENT ACCOUNTS
SEASONALLY ADJUSTED (£ MILLIONS)

	JAN	FEB	MAR	APR	MAY	JUN	JUL	AUG	SEP	OCT	NOV	DEC
1919	962	944	978	986	996	1091	1001	1016	1035	1039	1066	1072
1920	1109	1129	1143	1147	1103	1082	1068	1085	1078	1087	1076	1065
1921	1075	1059	1031	1014	1022	1010	1014	1013	1016	1035	1009	999
1922	1014	1037	1015	1013	1021	993	994	986	967	989	986	966
1923	993	989	976	983	976	966	962	952	946	950	944	951
1924	953	950	960	963	965	961	945	939	948	942	938	940
1925	934	947	947	928	908	917	907	910	914	918	921	920
1926	913	922	924	917	919	925	921	929	912	927	922	926
1927	916	917	922	926	931	943	928	937	937	952	936	940
1928	945	943	945	954	952	958	958	951	949	956	951	981
1929	966	961	956	955	942	951	945	934	934	919	905	916
1930	897	888	901	923	920	935	926	923	941	927	927	948
1931	940	926	920	908	910	932	925	895	888	857	873	830
1932	799	786	821	808	831	851	893	904	910	912	927	947
1933	958	968	962	973	987	986	982	997	987	981	982	970
1934	952	944	935	942	949	935	950	946	951	958	977	998
1935	1010	1023	1026	1029	1041	1051	1072	1076	1084	1062	1083	1090
1936	1102	1101	1116	1134	1147	1152	1170	1180	1191	1195	1203	1191

TABLE 6.12 : LONDON CLEARING BANKS DEPOSIT ACCOUNTS (£ MILLIONS)

	JAN	FEB	MAR	APR	MAY	JUN	JUL	AUG	SEP	OCT	NOV	DEC
1919	443	452	457	472	484	514	493	500	504	529	535	555
1920	573	570	574	589	597	615	635	644	646	667	671	684
1921	694	697	692	708	719	735	744	738	741	757	759	763
1922	763	756	729	732	729	730	706	688	675	675	667	660
1923	655	647	630	635	637	643	645	644	649	659	667	670
1924	677	670	656	660	661	667	667	662	660	666	671	671
1925	669	678	662	682	688	688	691	683	685	681	678	676
1926	672	675	666	675	671	685	689	691	694	700	711	721
1927	725	724	715	722	720	728	716	719	721	733	742	752
1928	749	738	729	736	736	753	760	763	763	768	778	789
1929	787	796	781	785	790	795	795	798	798	814	819	815
1930	814	803	781	797	820	827	828	821	821	838	844	847
1931	842	829	798	784	789	791	787	777	769	797	841	846
1932	831	838	832	845	854	876	873	908	921	932	929	963
1933	953	947	935	939	938	942	933	928	924	916	905	900
1934	893	881	880	890	887	888	874	869	873	885	900	910
1935	899	898	886	895	897	907	899	899	903	921	918	924
1936	906	909	920	942	959	962	954	958	967	966	973	979

TABLE 6.13 : LONDON CLEARING BANKS DEPOSIT ACCOUNTS
SEASONALLY ADJUSTED (£ MILLIONS)

	JAN	FEB	MAR	APR	MAY	JUN	JUL	AUG	SEP	OCT	NOV	DEC
1919	440	452	464	475	486	512	494	503	507	527	530	547
1920	569	569	583	593	599	612	636	648	650	664	665	675
1921	689	696	703	713	722	732	745	742	746	754	752	753
1922	757	755	740	737	732	727	707	692	680	672	661	651
1923	650	646	640	639	640	640	646	648	654	656	661	661
1924	672	669	666	664	664	664	668	666	665	663	665	662
1925	664	677	672	687	691	685	692	687	690	678	672	667
1926	667	674	676	679	674	682	690	695	699	697	705	711
1927	720	723	726	727	723	725	717	723	726	730	736	742
1928	743	737	740	741	739	750	761	767	768	765	771	778
1929	781	795	793	790	793	791	796	802	804	811	812	804
1930	808	802	793	802	823	823	829	826	827	834	837	835
1931	836	828	810	789	792	787	788	781	774	794	834	834
1932	825	837	845	851	857	872	874	913	927	928	921	950
1933	946	946	949	945	942	938	935	933	930	912	897	888
1934	886	880	893	896	891	884	875	874	879	881	892	898
1935	892	897	900	901	901	903	901	904	909	917	910	911
1936	899	908	934	948	963	958	956	963	974	962	965	966

TABLE 6.14 : LONDON CLEARING BANKS TOTAL DEPOSITS (£ MILLIONS)

	JAN	FEB	MAR	APR	MAY	JUN	JUL	AUG	SEP	OCT	NOV	DEC
1921				1752	1771	1811	1829	1807	1815	1846	1838	1863
1922	1872	1848	1791	1782	1790	1800	1774	1732	1704	1729	1711	1728
1923	1736	1687	1639	1649	1650	1680	1680	1653	1651	1670	1671	1714
1924	1715	1673	1643	1655	1658	1692	1682	1656	1652	1674	1667	1697
1925	1693	1683	1644	1645	1627	1663	1671	1649	1651	1665	1656	1684
1926	1675	1644	1625	1628	1637	1668	1684	1671	1660	1686	1685	1726
1927	1731	1690	1669	1679	1687	1722	1719	1706	1705	1747	1731	1766
1928	1748	1734	1709	1728	1725	1773	1786	1768	1769	1790	1789	1843
1929	1846	1814	1777	1781	1770	1808	1816	1796	1792	1803	1789	1811
1930	1805	1751	1719	1750	1780	1829	1831	1804	1800	1828	1838	1876
1931	1873	1820	1764	1736	1738	1782	1788	1745	1712	1724	1706	1737
1932	1714	1658	1676	1681	1699	1764	1804	1851	1865	1893	1898	1983
1933	1983	1957	1925	1930	1944	1978	1973	1966	1958	1951	1928	1941
1934	1920	1867	1831	1852	1858	1870	1871	1856	1858	1891	1911	1971
1935	1982	1954	1923	1940	1961	2003	2019	2013	2024	2036	2039	2091
1936	2092	2053	2038	2083	2113	2155	2170	2171	2180	2201	2209	2237
1937	2230	2199	2169	2178	2180	2216	2216	2205	2208	2234	2231	2250
1938	2248	2200	2177	2191	2185	2221	2230	2219	2190	2176	2168	2172
1939	2148	2096	2074	2077	2088	2137	2158	2162	2185	2241	2257	2350

TABLE 6.15 : LONDON CLEARING BANKS TOTAL DEPOSITS
SEASONALLY ADJUSTED (£ MILLIONS)

	JAN	FEB	MAR	APR	MAY	JUN	JUL	AUG	SEP	OCT	NOV	DEC
1921				1780	1796	1801	1818	1814	1826	1837	1835	1822
1922	1835	1852	1826	1810	1815	1790	1764	1738	1714	1721	1708	1690
1923	1702	1690	1671	1675	1673	1671	1670	1659	1661	1662	1668	1677
1924	1681	1676	1675	1681	1682	1683	1672	1662	1662	1666	1664	1660
1925	1660	1686	1675	1671	1660	1654	1662	1655	1661	1657	1653	1648
1926	1642	1647	1656	1653	1650	1659	1674	1677	1670	1678	1682	1688
1927	1697	1693	1702	1706	1711	1713	1709	1712	1715	1739	1728	1728
1928	1714	1738	1742	1755	1750	1764	1776	1775	1780	1781	1785	1803
1929	1810	1818	1811	1809	1795	1798	1805	1803	1803	1794	1786	1771
1930	1769	1754	1753	1777	1805	1820	1820	1810	1811	1819	1835	1835
1931	1836	1823	1798	1763	1763	1772	1777	1751	1722	1716	1703	1699
1932	1680	1661	1709	1707	1723	1755	1793	1857	1876	1884	1895	1940
1933	1944	1961	1962	1960	1972	1968	1962	1973	1970	1941	1925	1899
1934	1882	1871	1867	1881	1884	1860	1860	1863	1869	1882	1908	1928
1935	1943	1958	1960	1971	1989	1992	2007	2020	2036	2026	2035	2045
1936	2051	2057	2078	2116	2143	2144	2157	2179	2193	2190	2205	2188
1937	2186	2203	2211	2212	2211	2204	2203	2213	2221	2223	2227	2201
1938	2204	2204	2219	2225	2216	2209	2217	2227	2203	2165	2164	2125
1939	2106	2100	2114	2109	2118	2126	2145	2170	2198	2230	2253	2299

TABLE 6.16 : NET CIRCULATION OF CURRENCY (£MILLIONS)

	JAN	FEB	MAR	APR	MAY	JUN	JUL	AUG	SEP	OCT	NOV	DEC
1921	457	447	446	442	437	431	427	423	414	412	412	424
1922	407	400	398	398	395	403	394	391	384	384	383	396
1923	380	376	378	382	381	393	388	386	379	377	378	389
1924	379	376	380	386	385	392	392	389	383	382	381	387
1925	376	372	375	382	378	380	380	379	372	370	371	382
1926	367	362	368	373	380	375	376	373	365	364	363	377
1927	360	355	359	367	365	370	372	370	362	364	363	381
1928	361	354	356	364	362	372	368	365	359	359	355	369
1929	355	350	354	359	356	370	365	363	358	356	353	362
1930	351	344	349	355	355	364	362	361	355	353	353	362
1931	333	329	333	341	339	339	345	345	345	346	347	359
1932	342	340	350	349	349	349	354	354	346	346	348	362
1933	349	346	350	357	356	357	360	360	354	354	354	367
1934	352	350	356	360	362	362	368	368	362	363	361	379
1935	361	358	363	374	373	379	384	383	380	381	382	401
1936	380	378	384	396	402	412	420	423	424	422	423	444
1937	430	436	447	445	454	459	471	471	466	464	462	476
1938	456	455	460	471	463	465	467	462	460	466	460	473
1939	449	447	454	467	470	468	478	483	498	496	499	518

TABLE 6.17 : NET CIRCULATION OF CURRENCY (£ MILLIONS) SEASONALLY ADJUSTED

	JAN	FEB	MAR	APR	MAY	JUN	JUL	AUG	SEP	OCT	NOV	DEC
1921	464	459	452	441	437	426	421	418	415	414	415	412
1922	414	410	404	397	395	398	388	387	385	386	385	385
1923	386	386	383	381	381	388	382	382	380	379	380	378
1924	385	386	385	385	385	387	386	385	384	384	383	376
1925	382	382	380	381	378	376	374	375	373	371	373	371
1926	373	372	373	372	380	371	370	369	366	365	365	367
1927	366	364	364	366	365	366	366	366	363	365	365	370
1928	367	363	361	363	362	368	362	361	360	360	357	359
1929	361	359	359	358	356	366	360	359	359	357	355	352
1930	357	353	354	354	355	360	357	357	356	354	355	352
1931	338	338	338	341	339	335	340	341	346	347	349	349
1932	348	349	355	348	349	345	349	350	347	347	350	352
1933	355	355	355	356	356	353	355	356	355	355	356	357
1934	358	359	361	359	362	358	362	364	363	364	363	369
1935	367	367	368	373	373	375	378	379	381	383	384	390
1936	386	388	389	395	402	407	414	418	425	424	426	432
1937	437	447	453	444	454	454	464	466	467	466	465	463
1938	463	467	466	470	463	460	460	457	461	468	463	460
1939	456	459	460	466	470	463	471	478	500	498	502	504

TABLE 6.18 : BANKERS DEPOSITS AT THE BANK OF ENGLAND (£ MILLIONS)

	JAN	FEB	MAR	APR	MAY	JUN	JUL	AUG	SEP	OCT	NOV	DEC
1920	89	79	83	88	68	98	81	79	75	87	74	102
1921	89	78	74	80	76	92	92	81	86	109	82	91
1922	95	97	80	83	83	78	77	69	72	76	71	80
1923	86	68	65	70	65	70	74	67	66	65	64	81
1924	77	66	65	66	64	77	71	66	69	67	65	87
1925	70	74	70	70	65	74	78	68	70	65	68	86
1926	71	66	63	65	67	78	72	68	66	67	63	77
1927	78	66	64	64	63	68	68	65	63	64	61	73
1928	76	61	64	60	61	68	75	65	66	63	62	69
1929	68	62	62	63	60	64	65	61	65	64	58	63
1930	76	56	60	65	61	63	70	63	66	61	58	81
1931	64	60	61	57	58	69	69	59	60	68	60	87
1932	76	71	75	72	76	85	85	84	86	80	87	98
1933	114	93	100	101	92	102	95	90	103	108	103	101
1934	116	97	103	104	105	98	99	87	94	104	98	98
1935	108	99	104	103	102	103	100	90	93	79	91	88
1936	115	105	93	100	83	90	95	97	94	84	94	101
1937	104	97	85	93	93	111	95	93	104	93	88	107
1938	123	107	113	109	98	111	113	104	98	99	100	101
1939	123	107	101	94	99	100	93	90	109	114	104	101

TABLE 6.19 : BANKERS DEPOSITS AT THE BANK OF ENGLAND
SEASONALLY ADJUSTED (£ MILLIONS)

	JAN	FEB	MAR	APR	MAY	JUN	JUL	AUG	SEP	OCT	NOV	DEC
1920	80	80	86	90	71	94	78	83	77	88	79	92
1921	80	80	77	82	80	88	89	85	88	111	88	82
1922	86	99	83	84	88	75	74	73	74	77	76	72
1923	77	69	67	71	69	67	72	70	67	67	68	73
1924	69	67	67	67	67	74	69	69	70	68	70	79
1925	63	75	72	71	69	71	75	72	72	66	72	78
1926	63	67	65	66	71	75	70	72	67	68	67	70
1927	70	67	67	66	66	66	66	68	65	66	65	67
1928	68	62	66	61	64	66	73	68	67	64	66	62
1929	61	63	64	64	63	61	63	65	67	65	62	57
1930	68	57	62	67	64	61	68	66	68	62	62	74
1931	58	61	63	58	61	66	67	62	62	70	64	79
1932	68	72	78	74	81	82	83	88	88	81	93	89
1933	102	95	104	103	97	98	92	95	105	111	110	92
1934	104	99	107	107	110	94	96	91	96	106	104	89
1935	97	101	107	105	108	99	97	95	95	81	97	79
1936	103	107	96	102	87	86	92	102	97	85	101	92
1937	93	98	88	95	99	107	92	98	106	95	94	97
1938	110	108	117	111	103	107	110	110	100	101	106	91
1939	110	108	105	96	104	96	91	95	111	116	110	91

7 Interest Rates

TABLES

SOURCES

Tables 7.1–7.3 *Bankers', Insurance Managers' and Agents' Magazine*
Tables 7.4 and 7.6 *London and Cambridge Economic Service Bulletin*
Table 7.5 *Statistical Abstract of the United Kingdom* and *Bank of England Statistical Summary*
Table 7.7 A. L. Bowley, G. L. Schwartz and K. C. Smith, *A New Index of Prices of Securities*, LCES Special Memorandum 33 (London, 1931), and *London and Cambridge Economic Service Bulletin*

Interest rate series are among the few which are readily available in a consistent form over a substantial number of years. Tables 7.1–7.4 present some of the more important short rate series, and Tables 7.5–7.7 provide some measures of long rates.

Tables 7.1–7.3 show mid-month observations of the discount rate charged on the best type of bills in the London discount market. Quotations for each year appeared in the January issue of the 'Monetary Review' section of the *Bankers', Insurance Managers' and Agents' Magazine* and these are reproduced here. Where more than one quotation appeared, the lower has always been used. The Index of the short money rate appeared regularly in the *London and Cambridge Economic Service Bulletin*; it was an average of the discount rate charged by the Bank of England (bank rate), the bankers' deposit rate, the discount market rate on best three-month bills, and the day-to-day rate. The deposit, day-to-day, and market bill rates were those for the week ending the fifteenth of the month. Until February 1929 the original index was tied to the base 1913 average = 100; and from that date was on a 1924 base. In the table presented here the earlier figures have been converted to the 1924 base – i.e., the earlier data have been multiplied by the ratio of the arithmetic mean of the twelve observations for 1924 on the old basis to the arithmetic mean of the same observations on the new basis.

Of the long-term rates the most straightforward is the yield on $2\frac{1}{2}$ per cent Consols presented in Table 7.5. The Bank of England's figures for 1931 onwards were 'averages of mid-day quotations . . . with allowance for accrued interest' but before deduction for tax. When below par 'a flat yield' was taken, irrespective of price. The other two long-term indices were compiled by the London and Cambridge Economic Service as part of their much broader coverage of the capital market. The index appearing in Table 7.6 averaged the yield on four fixed-interest securities. These were $3\frac{1}{2}$ per cent London County Council, three per cent local loans, Metropolitan Water Board B, and the four per cent funding loan. Until December 1922 quotations for the last working day of the month were used, and thereafter mid-month quotations. The index was modified in 1931 by A. L. Bowley, G. L. Schwartz and K. C. Smith. The composition of the securities used was changed to the following four: three per cent London County Council, four per cent London Midland and Scottish Railway debentures, the $3\frac{1}{2}$ per cent conversion loan, and the four per cent funding loan. It was also converted to a 1924 base and the series pushed back to 1925. The authors believed the differences between the two series to have been 'insignificant in most months'.[1]

NOTE

1 LCES Special Memorandum 33, p. 13.

TABLE 7.1 : MARKET RATE OF INTEREST ON BEST THREE-MONTH BILLS
(PERCENTAGE PER ANNUM)

	JAN	FEB	MAR	APR	MAY	JUN	JUL	AUG	SEP	OCT	NOV	DEC
1919	3.5	3.5	3.5	3.5	3.5	3.1	3.5	3.6	3.7	4.5	5.9	5.9
1920	5.5	5.9	5.7	6.6	6.7	6.4	6.5	6.6	6.7	6.6	6.6	6.7
1921	6.6	6.7	6.2	6.1	5.7	5.5	4.6	4.7	4.1	3.9	3.9	3.4
1922	3.7	3.1	3.4	2.5	2.3	2.4	1.8	2.4	2.4	2.3	2.4	2.6
1923	2.1	2.4	2.1	2.0	2.1	2.1	3.2	3.1	3.2	3.1	3.3	3.2
1924	3.4	3.6	3.1	3.0	2.9	2.9	3.7	3.7	3.7	3.7	3.7	3.7
1925	3.7	3.7	4.4	4.2	4.6	4.4	4.2	3.7	3.5	3.7	3.9	4.8
1926	4.7	4.2	4.4	4.3	4.2	4.2	4.3	4.5	4.5	4.7	4.6	4.5
1927	4.0	4.2	4.3	3.8	3.7	4.3	4.3	4.3	4.3	4.2	4.3	4.3
1928	3.9	4.1	4.1	4.0	4.0	3.7	4.0	4.2	4.2	4.4	4.4	4.3
1929	4.2	5.2	5.3	5.1	5.2	5.3	5.3	5.4	4.6	6.1	4.9	4.8
1930	4.0	3.9	2.4	2.5	2.2	2.4	2.4	2.2	2.1	2.1	2.2	2.4
1931	2.2	2.6	2.6	2.6	2.1	2.1	3.4	4.2	5.5	5.6	5.7	5.6
1932	5.0	4.2	2.2	2.0	1.2	1.0	0.8	0.6	0.6	0.8	0.9	1.3
1933	0.9	0.9	0.6	0.5	0.5	0.6	0.4	0.4	0.4	0.8	1.1	1.1
1934	1.0	0.9	0.9	0.9	0.9	0.9	0.9	0.8	0.6	0.8	0.4	0.6
1935	0.3	0.3	0.6	0.6	0.6	0.8	0.6	0.6	0.6	0.6	0.6	0.8
1936	0.6	0.6	0.6	0.6	0.6	0.9	0.6	0.6	0.5	0.6	0.6	1.1
1937	0.6	0.5	0.5	0.5	0.5	0.7	0.5	0.5	0.5	0.5	0.6	0.7
1938	0.5	0.5	0.5	0.5	0.5	0.6	0.5	0.5	1.0	0.8	0.8	1.0
1939	0.5	0.5	0.5	1.5	0.6	0.8	0.8	0.8	3.5	1.9	1.2	1.2

TABLE 7.2 : MARKET RATE OF INTEREST ON BEST FOUR-MONTH BILLS
(PERCENTAGE PER ANNUM)

	JAN	FEB	MAR	APR	MAY	JUN	JUL	AUG	SEP	OCT	NOV	DEC
1919	3.5	3.5	3.5	3.5	3.5	3.2	3.6	3.7	3.9	4.6	5.9	5.9
1920	5.4	5.9	5.9	6.6	6.8	6.6	6.5	6.6	6.9	6.7	6.7	6.6
1921	6.6	6.5	6.2	6.0	5.7	5.5	4.6	4.7	4.3	3.9	3.9	3.4
1922	3.8	3.1	3.4	2.5	2.3	2.4	1.9	2.5	2.6	2.4	2.4	2.6
1923	2.1	2.4	2.2	2.0	2.1	2.1	3.2	3.2	3.5	3.1	3.4	3.2
1924	3.4	3.6	3.2	3.1	3.0	3.0	3.7	3.8	3.9	3.7	3.7	3.8
1925	3.8	3.7	4.5	4.3	4.6	4.4	4.2	3.8	3.7	3.7	3.9	4.8
1926	4.7	4.2	4.4	4.3	4.2	4.2	4.3	4.2	4.6	4.7	4.7	4.5
1927	4.0	4.2	4.3	3.8	3.7	4.3	4.3	4.3	4.3	4.3	4.3	4.3
1928	3.9	4.1	4.1	4.0	4.1	3.7	4.1	4.2	4.2	4.4	4.4	4.4
1929	4.3	5.2	5.3	5.1	5.2	5.4	5.4	5.6	5.7	6.1	4.9	4.7
1930	4.0	3.9	2.6	2.6	2.3	2.6	2.4	2.3	2.2	2.2	2.2	2.5
1931	2.2	2.7	2.7	2.6	2.1	2.2	3.4	4.4	6.0	5.9	5.9	5.7
1932	5.4	4.4	2.4	2.1	1.2	1.1	0.9	0.8	1.0	0.9	1.0	1.4
1933	0.9	0.9	0.7	0.6	0.6	0.6	0.5	0.4	0.5	0.9	1.1	1.2
1934	1.1	0.9	0.9	1.0	0.9	0.9	0.9	0.8	0.8	0.8	0.4	0.6
1935	0.4	0.4	0.6	0.6	0.6	0.8	0.6	0.6	0.3	0.7	0.6	0.8
1936	0.6	0.6	0.6	0.6	0.6	0.9	0.6	0.6	0.6	0.6	0.6	1.0
1937	0.6	0.6	0.6	0.6	0.6	0.8	0.6	0.6	0.6	0.6	0.6	0.7
1938	0.5	0.5	0.5	0.5	0.5	0.6	0.5	0.5	1.1	0.8	0.8	1.0
1939	0.6	0.6	0.6	1.6	0.7	0.9	0.8	0.8	4.5	2.0	1.2	1.2

TABLE 7.3 : MARKET RATE OF INTEREST ON BEST SIX-MONTH BILLS (PERCENTAGE PER ANNUM)

	JAN	FEB	MAR	APR	MAY	JUN	JUL	AUG	SEP	OCT	NOV	DEC
1919	3.5	3.5	3.5	3.6	3.6	3.2	4.0	4.0	4.1	5.0	5.9	5.9
1920	5.5	5.9	6.0	6.8	6.9	6.9	6.9	6.9	6.9	6.9	6.7	6.6
1921	6.6	6.1	6.0	5.9	5.7	5.5	4.7	5.0	4.5	4.0	4.0	3.4
1922	3.8	3.1	3.4	2.5	2.3	2.5	2.0	2.5	2.6	2.6	2.7	2.7
1923	2.4	2.6	2.4	2.1	2.2	2.2	3.7	3.7	3.7	3.4	3.5	3.4
1924	3.5	3.6	3.4	3.2	3.1	3.1	4.0	4.1	4.1	3.9	3.9	3.9
1925	4.0	3.9	4.6	4.5	4.7	4.6	4.4	4.1	3.9	4.0	4.0	4.8
1926	4.7	4.1	4.2	4.3	4.2	4.2	4.3	4.6	4.6	4.8	4.7	4.5
1927	4.0	4.2	4.2	3.8	3.7	4.4	4.4	4.4	4.4	4.4	4.4	4.3
1928	3.9	4.1	4.1	4.1	4.1	3.9	4.1	4.4	4.4	4.4	4.4	4.4
1929	4.4	5.3	5.4	5.2	5.3	5.4	5.5	5.9	6.0	6.1	4.9	4.7
1930	4.0	3.9	2.6	2.7	2.6	2.6	2.7	2.6	2.4	2.2	2.3	2.5
1931	2.4	2.9	2.8	2.7	2.2	2.2	4.2	4.7	6.2	6.0	6.0	6.0
1932	5.6	4.6	2.5	2.2	1.5	1.2	1.1	1.1	1.1	1.1	1.1	1.4
1933	1.0	1.0	0.9	0.8	0.8	0.8	0.8	0.7	0.7	0.9	1.2	1.2
1934	1.1	1.1	1.0	1.1	1.0	1.0	1.1	1.0	0.9	0.9	0.5	0.6
1935	0.5	0.4	0.7	0.7	0.6	0.8	0.8	0.7	0.7	0.8	0.7	0.8
1936	0.6	0.6	0.6	0.6	0.6	0.9	0.8	0.6	0.6	0.6	0.6	0.9
1937	0.6	0.6	0.6	0.6	0.6	0.8	0.7	0.6	0.6	0.6	0.6	0.6
1938	0.6	0.6	0.6	0.6	0.6	0.6	0.6	0.6	1.2	0.9	0.8	0.9
1939	0.6	0.6	0.6	2.0	1.0	1.0	1.0	1.0	5.0	2.5	1.5	1.5

TABLE 7.4 : INDEX OF SHORT MONEY RATE (1924 AVERAGE = 100)

	JAN	FEB	MAR	APR	MAY	JUN	JUL	AUG	SEP	OCT	NOV	DEC
1919	121.6	124.2	118.9	121.6	121.6	115.0	113.7	124.2	125.5	134.6	169.9	155.5
1920	160.8	169.9	160.8	176.5	197.4	192.1	197.4	192.1	201.3	197.4	201.3	197.4
1921	197.4	211.7	201.3	197.4	176.5	181.7	160.8	150.3	132.0	138.5	129.4	117.6
1922	117.6	111.1	112.4	91.5	83.7	81.0	62.7	66.7	70.6	66.7	71.9	66.7
1923	62.7	69.3	69.3	68.0	64.0	62.7	100.6	95.4	98.0	98.0	99.3	91.5
1924	95.4	103.3	95.4	95.4	94.1	90.2	100.6	107.2	104.6	104.6	105.9	103.3
1925	105.9	105.9	133.3	135.9	142.5	134.6	133.3	122.9	116.3	104.6	111.1	138.5
1926	142.5	137.2	139.9	137.2	137.2	134.6	137.2	135.9	137.2	141.2	139.9	137.2
1927	132.0	133.3	137.2	135.9	118.9	124.2	124.2	126.8	125.5	125.5	125.5	125.5
1928	122.9	124.2	125.5	124.2	122.9	116.3	120.2	124.2	125.5	129.4	125.5	122.9
1929	125.0	162.0	160.0	158.0	159.0	156.0	160.0	156.0	157.0	189.0	177.0	151.0
1930	136.0	125.0	104.0	82.0	68.0	71.0	69.0	69.0	65.0	65.0	70.0	66.0

TABLE 7.5 : YIELD ON 2.5% CONSOLS (PERCENTAGE PER ANNUM)

	JAN	FEB	MAR	APR	MAY	JUN	JUL	AUG	SEP	OCT	NOV	DEC
1919	4.2	4.2	4.3	4.5	4.5	4.7	4.8	4.8	4.9	4.8	4.9	4.9
1920	4.9	5.0	5.2	5.4	5.2	5.3	5.3	5.4	5.4	5.4	5.6	5.7
1921	5.3	5.3	5.3	5.2	5.3	5.4	5.2	5.2	5.2	5.1	5.1	5.0
1922	4.9	4.7	4.5	4.2	4.3	4.4	4.3	4.3	4.4	4.4	4.4	4.5
1923	4.5	4.4	4.2	4.2	4.3	4.3	4.3	4.3	4.3	4.3	4.4	4.5
1924	4.5	4.4	4.5	4.4	4.3	4.4	4.4	4.4	4.4	4.4	4.3	4.3
1925	4.3	4.3	4.4	4.4	4.4	4.5	4.4	4.4	4.5	4.5	4.5	4.5
1926	4.5	4.5	4.6	4.6	4.5	4.5	4.5	4.5	4.6	4.6	4.6	4.6
1927	4.5	4.5	4.5	4.6	4.5	4.6	4.6	4.6	4.6	4.5	4.5	4.6
1928	4.5	4.5	4.5	4.4	4.4	4.5	4.5	4.5	4.5	4.5	4.5	4.5
1929	4.4	4.5	4.5	4.5	4.6	4.6	4.6	4.6	4.7	4.7	4.7	4.7
1930	4.6	4.6	4.5	4.5	4.5	4.5	4.5	4.5	4.5	4.4	4.3	4.3
1931	4.3	4.4	4.4	4.3	4.2	4.2	4.2	4.4	4.5	4.5	4.6	4.7
1932	4.5	4.5	4.2	4.1	4.0	3.9	3.5	3.5	3.4	3.3	3.4	3.4
1933	3.4	3.3	3.4	3.3	3.4	3.4	3.5	3.4	3.4	3.4	3.4	3.4
1934	3.3	3.3	3.1	3.1	3.2	3.2	3.1	3.1	3.1	3.1	2.8	2.8
1935	2.7	2.8	2.9	2.9	2.8	2.9	2.9	2.9	3.0	3.0	3.0	2.9
1936	2.9	2.9	2.9	2.9	2.9	2.9	2.9	3.0	2.9	2.9	2.9	3.0
1937	3.0	3.1	3.3	3.3	3.3	3.3	3.4	3.4	3.4	3.4	3.3	3.4
1938	3.3	3.2	3.4	3.4	3.4	3.4	3.3	3.3	3.5	3.5	3.5	3.6
1939	3.6	3.6	3.6	3.8	3.7	3.7	3.7	3.9	4.0	3.8	3.7	3.7

TABLE 7.6 : INDEX OF THE YIELD ON FOUR FIXED-INTEREST SECURITIES
(1913 AVERAGE = 100)

	JAN	FEB	MAR	APR	MAY	JUN	JUL	AUG	SEP	OCT	NOV	DEC
1919	126	127	130	130	130	135	139	143	144	141	144	145
1920	145	148	159	160	157	158	155	158	159	162	163	161
1921	156	155	154	151	150	152	152	152	152	152	150	140
1922	139	131	128	124	123	124	123	125	129	128	126	127
1923	125	123	123	120	118	117	123	120	119	120	125	126
1924	129	127	126	124	123	123	124	124	123	123	121	122
1925	122	121	123	123	124	126	126	123	125	125	126	128
1926	127	127	128	129	127	126	126	127	129	130	129	129
1927	126	126	127	127	126	127	127	127	127	127	127	127
1928	124	125	124	123	123	123	123	124	124	124	123	123
1929	122											

TABLE 7.7 : INDEX OF THE YIELD OF FIXED-INTEREST SECURITIES
(1924 AVERAGE = 100)

	JAN	FEB	MAR	APR	MAY	JUN	JUL	AUG	SEP	OCT	NOV	DEC
1925	99.4	99.3	100.4	100.5	100.6	103.4	101.9	100.4	104.2	104.5	103.4	103.9
1926	103.2	102.9	103.8	104.1	102.9	102.4	103.4	103.8	104.6	105.1	104.8	104.3
1927	101.9	102.8	103.9	103.8	103.1	103.6	104.1	103.3	103.2	102.8	103.2	102.3
1928	101.5	101.9	100.9	99.1	99.7	100.0	100.7	101.4	101.5	101.8	101.4	99.9
1929	98.9	101.9	102.9	102.3	102.9	103.5	104.0	106.2	107.0	106.5	106.3	105.8
1930	104.7	104.2	102.0	99.7	101.7	102.4	100.4	100.9	100.4	98.7	96.3	96.9
1931	96.8	101.8	100.6	99.9	97.6	96.0	98.7	101.3	102.9	108.1	106.5	111.2
1932	107.5	107.2	97.0	96.0	91.7	92.5	82.7	83.9	82.7	79.0	81.8	81.9
1933	82.2	81.3	82.1	80.2	81.5	81.5	82.5	80.7	79.3	79.3	79.4	78.4
1934	77.4	77.7	76.6	76.6	76.7	76.9	76.2	75.8	75.5	75.0	71.1	72.6
1935	71.4	73.4	73.5	74.1	72.9	73.8	72.9	73.0	75.0	76.5	73.5	73.5
1936	73.0	73.2	73.6	72.9	72.8	73.8	73.9	73.3	73.1	72.4	72.8	74.0
1937	74.5	77.6	79.2	78.6	78.2	79.0	79.3	79.5	79.9	79.4	77.5	78.1
1938	77.1	77.1	78.8	77.8	78.4	78.5	76.9	77.9	81.0	80.9	80.9	82.3
1939	82.5	84.2	83.2	87.6	86.1	85.6	85.9	86.6	90.0	90.1	86.3	86.1

8 Capital

TABLES

SOURCES

Tables 8.1–8.2 *Midland Bank Review*
Tables 8.3–8.4 *London and Cambridge Economic Service Bulletin*
Tables 8.5–8.8 *Bankers', Insurance Managers' and Agents' Magazine*
Table 8.9 *The Economist*

The figures for capital issues and the prices of various securities are all presented in monthly form. There are two series on new capital issues, three price indices of securities and a securities values index, subdivided into fixed and variable. In addition to this there is an index of profits.

First, the only difference between the two new issues series is that one is for the United Kingdom alone and the other includes issues for abroad. The figures in these series can be taken as a conservative total of new capital raised through the particular medium of the issue market. They exclude borrowing by the British Government for national purposes, vendors' and bonus shares, issues for conversion or redemption of securities previously held in the United Kingdom, short-dated bills sold in anticipation of long-term borrowings and loans by local authorities except when there is a specified limit to the total subscription. They do not include issues of capital by private companies unless particulars of these were publicly announced. The statistics represent not the nominal amount of the issues, but the total sums raised, as computed from prices of subscription.

The price index of fixed-interest securities was based on quotations of four 'gilt-edged' securities, all practically irredeemable. Mid-month quotations were used. The attempt being made was to represent 'pure interest', the consideration of long-term investors, uncomplicated by redemption factors and industrial or speculative vicissitudes. The index for twenty industrials was based on the quotation of the ordinary shares of twenty long-established British Companies (in 1920 the companies included Cammel Laird, Harrods, Vickers, Cunard and so on[1]), in good standing and operating with considerable capital. They were chosen to represent different classes of industry and commerce. For contemporaries it was one of four series taken to represent the general index of business conditions. The new index of security prices replaced the above index that was based on companies that had been of importance in 1913; and the relative importance assigned to industries had been derived from the 1907 census of production. By the end of the 1920s the magnitude of the fluctuations in this index were not being captured with sufficient precision, dominated as they were by the very variable fortunes of a few companies. The new index-number was based on the quotation of ordinary shares of ninety-two industrial companies operating wholly or principally in the United Kingdom. The basis of selection was industrial importance, good standing and stable financial organisation. Banks and railways were excluded on the ground that the course followed by their shares was uncommon. Weights were assigned to the companies in proportion to the total value of the particular shares at the average of the four mid-quarterly market quotations in 1924. Series were then computed for each month.[2]

The securities values index was made up of a total of 365 stocks and shares and subdivided into two groups of fixed and variable securities. The fixed had eighty-seven securities and the variable 278 and the more important of these were as follows:

Fixed:	
British and Indian funds	10
Colonial government stock	8
Foreign government stock	26
Corporation stocks (colonial and foreign)	15
	59 of the 87 securities
Variable:	
Indian railway stocks	5
British bank shares	13
Brewery stocks	10
South African mines	19
Commercial and industrial shares	38
Foreign railways	20
Insurance shares	17
Colonial and foreign bank shares	18
U. S. railway shares	11
	151 of the 278 securities

The index of profit is that of *The Economist* and first appeared in 1939. Before 1939 *The Economist* published an unweighted quarterly index showing relative changes in *reported* company profits, after deduction of debenture interest payments, and compared the current quarter with its corresponding quarter of the previous year. The new index tried to overcome the problems of sharp oscillations associated with dependence on one quarter's figures by averaging all the previous four quarters. Thus the new index shown here is an average of the unweighted index numbers for each of the preceding four quarters, now weighted in proportion to the total profit reported in each of these quarters. 'Thus each quarterly index number embraces the profits reported in the latest quarter; but it is not confined to them, and also includes the profits of the three preceding quarters.'[3] Therefore, *The Economist* believed it showed the 'proportion in which the profits reported in the last twelve months compared with the profits of similar periods in past years . . .'.[4] It is important to bear in mind that the figures refer only to reported profits and with no allowance for tax. In all some 2,000 companies were included by *The Economist*.

NOTES

1 Full description in *London and Cambridge Economic Service Bulletin*, II, 1, p. 15.

2 Further details are provided in LCES Special Memorandum 33.

3 *The Economist*, CXXXIV, January 14 1939, p. 61.

4 *Ibid*.

TABLE 8.1 : NEW CAPITAL ISSUES ON THE LONDON STOCK MARKET - TOTAL (£ MILLIONS)

	JAN	FEB	MAR	APR	MAY	JUN	JUL	AUG	SEP	OCT	NOV	DEC
1919	18.3	9.7	11.9	6.0	17.5	16.8	28.3	14.8	9.3	25.0	33.1	46.8
1920	42.4	35.2	69.4	45.8	20.9	27.6	43.4	9.9	20.1	28.1	33.0	8.5
1921	22.5	10.4	25.5	14.8	17.2	33.9	7.3	3.0	9.9	33.4	18.5	19.4
1922	42.3	26.0	24.9	17.2	35.8	22.0	18.6	1.1	5.2	25.3	9.7	7.5
1923	21.1	10.0	14.9	16.0	26.8	34.8	20.9	1.3	4.3	38.6	13.5	1.7
1924	11.5	22.4	13.3	4.8	34.8	19.3	21.4	3.6	7.9	37.0	21.4	26.1
1925	20.1	15.6	21.7	9.6	33.7	23.7	16.5	1.6	2.5	21.1	29.4	24.4
1926	28.4	25.8	23.9	13.5	10.9	29.2	26.7	1.5	15.9	29.2	28.1	20.2
1927	26.3	21.9	34.7	22.3	34.5	20.0	34.9	2.2	5.0	37.7	48.8	26.4
1928	33.8	27.9	41.7	18.6	39.3	41.4	41.8	6.5	18.3	40.6	28.0	24.7
1929	47.4	33.0	33.8	34.8	21.1	25.4	22.2	3.6	2.7	11.5	12.9	5.2
1930	16.9	26.2	26.3	21.3	37.9	13.2	16.4	6.6	5.0	30.5	19.9	15.8
1931	12.3	19.6	13.4	1.7	11.0	12.8	5.2	1.6	1.3	2.5	4.4	2.7
1932	2.9	12.0	12.1	18.0	12.3	17.5	3.3	0.0	0.0	19.7	10.8	4.3
1933	8.3	7.2	13.5	8.3	14.6	17.5	6.0	21.2	7.1	10.0	12.8	6.4
1934	10.9	7.0	7.1	9.6	22.4	12.0	15.0	9.9	6.7	23.5	13.0	13.0
1935	16.6	12.6	12.8	4.1	19.7	20.6	53.9	6.7	7.7	4.7	12.5	11.2
1936	33.9	19.7	7.0	10.4	19.5	18.4	24.4	6.1	9.5	26.9	20.9	20.2
1937	27.6	10.6	11.3	11.9	11.4	24.5	20.3	7.1	2.0	13.8	12.4	17.9
1938	7.4	19.2	6.4	5.0	27.4	8.5	15.2	2.2	1.6	2.6	12.8	9.6
1939	13.9	8.2	2.8	1.8	6.6	23.9	2.8	5.2	0.1	0.1	0.9	0.2

TABLE 8.2 : NEW CAPITAL ISSUES ON THE LONDON STOCK MARKET - BRITISH ONLY (£ MILLIONS)

	JAN	FEB	MAR	APR	MAY	JUN	JUL	AUG	SEP	OCT	NOV	DEC
1919	14.7	9.6	11.0	5.0	15.6	13.9	21.9	14.1	6.7	12.3	26.3	37.1
1920	30.1	31.9	65.1	44.7	19.1	21.3	41.7	6.5	18.4	24.2	23.4	4.8
1921	11.3	7.0	18.0	4.6	6.5	15.2	5.7	1.5	2.8	19.3	4.9	3.4
1922	27.4	6.6	9.6	5.9	9.0	6.0	12.1	0.8	4.7	7.7	5.6	5.0
1923	1.7	1.2	10.9	5.9	4.8	8.2	9.3	0.4	0.5	17.7	6.2	0.6
1924	5.6	5.5	6.6	2.9	5.5	13.7	12.3	1.2	5.3	9.4	11.0	10.3
1925	14.3	11.2	16.0	6.0	15.9	21.8	8.8	0.8	1.7	11.0	12.3	12.3
1926	9.5	22.3	12.3	6.5	4.3	13.5	15.9	0.8	8.7	13.9	18.7	14.4
1927	10.3	15.4	27.7	13.1	23.9	12.4	16.3	2.1	3.2	14.8	23.2	13.6
1928	14.2	22.6	18.7	10.6	25.8	25.4	24.1	5.5	7.6	29.7	17.0	18.0
1929	18.0	26.2	24.8	28.8	12.3	14.0	13.9	2.2	1.5	7.5	6.3	4.0
1930	11.3	8.0	16.9	11.9	17.8	7.7	13.1	3.5	2.4	12.8	11.5	10.4
1931	7.8	6.0	7.4	1.4	0.9	4.4	2.3	1.6	1.3	2.5	4.3	2.[illegible]
1932	0.3	9.1	11.1	9.6	8.9	15.4	3.2	0.0	0.0	11.8	10.3	4.[illegible]
1933	7.9	4.9	12.3	7.3	9.3	16.0	5.2	1.3	6.7	6.8	12.2	5.[illegible]
1934	8.7	5.3	6.0	8.7	11.4	7.0	10.0	3.2	5.6	20.8	11.0	9.[illegible]
1935	14.4	9.7	11.5	3.4	18.8	19.6	50.0	4.8	7.3	3.9	9.2	9.[illegible]
1936	33.0	18.5	6.9	8.8	17.2	15.3	20.7	4.3	8.0	22.7	18.3	17.[illegible]
1937	24.8	8.0	9.8	7.1	8.3	22.6	14.6	6.5	1.9	13.1	11.4	10.[illegible]
1938	6.5	13.8	6.3	4.7	16.6	8.1	11.2	1.8	1.6	1.8	10.9	9.[illegible]
1939	10.3	7.0	2.6	1.2	1.5	17.4	1.7	0.6	0.1	0.1	0.9	0.[illegible]

TABLE 8.3 : INDEX OF THE PRICE OF FIXED-INTEREST SECURITIES
(1924 AVERAGE = 100)

	JAN	FEB	MAR	APR	MAY	JUN	JUL	AUG	SEP	OCT	NOV	DEC
1925	100.6	100.7	99.6	99.5	99.4	96.7	98.1	99.6	96.2	95.9	96.8	96.2
1926	96.8	97.2	96.4	96.0	97.2	97.7	96.7	96.4	95.6	95.2	95.3	95.9
1927	98.1	96.7	96.3	96.2	97.1	96.5	96.1	96.8	96.9	97.2	96.9	97.8
1928	98.6	98.1	99.2	100.9	100.3	100.0	99.4	98.7	98.5	98.2	98.7	100.1
1929	101.1	98.2	97.1	97.9	97.2	97.3	96.0	94.2	93.5	93.9	94.1	94.5
1930	95.5	96.1	98.1	100.3	98.4	97.7	99.7	99.2	99.7	101.3	103.9	103.3
1931	103.5	98.5	99.6	100.2	103.0	104.6	101.5	99.2	97.9	92.6	94.0	90.2
1932	93.4	93.7	103.4	104.5	109.4	108.8	121.7	120.2	121.5	126.8	122.9	122.7
1933	122.3	123.6	122.4	125.3	123.1	123.1	121.6	124.3	126.2	126.3	126.4	127.5
1934	129.6	128.8	130.8	130.9	130.7	130.3	131.6	132.2	132.7	133.7	140.9	138.2
1935	140.4	136.9	136.5	135.3	137.6	135.9	137.6	137.5	132.6	131.0	136.4	136.4
1936	137.4	137.0	136.2	137.4	137.6	135.8	135.7	136.8	137.4	138.4	137.6	135.5
1937	134.5	129.2	126.3	127.3	127.8	126.7	126.1	126.0	125.2	126.1	129.0	128.2
1938	129.8	129.8	127.0	128.6	127.6	127.6	130.1	128.6	121.2	123.7	123.8	121.7
1939	121.4	119.2	120.5	114.3	116.2	117.2	116.7	115.7	111.2	111.0	116.0	116.6

TABLE 8.4 : INDEX OF THE PRICE ON TWENTY INDUSTRIAL SECURITIES
(1913 AVERAGE = 100)

	JAN	FEB	MAR	APR	MAY	JUN	JUL	AUG	SEP	OCT	NOV	DEC
1919	154	156	155	155	166	165	165	173	170	183	187	194
1920	214	205	199	189	175	162	160	152	155	156	138	129
1921	125	115	119	123	121	122	117	118	113	103	105	111
1922	112	118	119	130	133	133	136	138	136	139	144	150
1923	155	156	160	165	167	169	161	162	166	165	164	156
1924	155	164	158	159	158	156	155	158	158	160	172	172
1925	179	178	179	179	178	180	172	178	177	185	192	187
1926	191	187	182	177	182	186	181	184	187	190	197	192
1927	197	191	192	194	200	203	201	201	205	213	211	210
1928	216	217	225	239	246	240	241	243	248	249	245	239
1929	259											

TABLE 8.5 : INDEX OF SECURITY PRICES
(1924 AVERAGE = 100)

	JAN	FEB	MAR	APR	MAY	JUN	JUL	AUG	SEP	OCT	NOV	DEC
1925	110	108	108	107	106	106	103	108	109	112	116	113
1926	116	114	113	111	113	115	113	114	116	116	117	116
1927	120	119	119	119	122	122	122	124	126	131	131	131
1928	137	136	141	143	148	143	139	140	143	146	143	139
1929	149	148	143	143	144	141	138	142	144	135	121	121
1930	124	119	116	120	119	112	112	106	110	103	105	99
1931	96	94	96	94	80	82	86	82	78	87	92	81
1932	82	81	86	83	77	73	83	86	90	90	92	91
1933	95	96	92	93	96	101	108	106	110	115	114	113
1934	118	116	122	124	127	124	124	125	127	128	132	131
1935	137	133	130	131	137	141	141	148	141	139	149	147
1936	154	159	155	160	154	154	157	165	166	170	169	167
1937	169	165	156	156	154	148	150	152	146	139	138	133
1938	135	128	120	129	123	118	125	122	117	119	123	116
1939	115	118	126	115	119	118	115	118	106	104	106	105

TABLE 8.6 : INDEX OF THE VALUE OF FIXED-INTEREST SECURITIES
(DECEMBER 1921 = 100)

	JAN	FEB	MAR	APR	MAY	JUN	JUL	AUG	SEP	OCT	NOV	DEC
1922	102.5	107.3	108.0	112.9	112.7	112.0	113.2	113.1	111.2	112.1	111.0	111.0
1923	112.4	112.9	113.8	116.4	115.5	115.8	112.4	113.7	114.8	114.8	111.8	111.2
1924	109.6	111.3	111.7	113.6	113.1	113.4	112.6	113.0	113.1	113.5	113.2	112.9
1925	111.8	112.4	111.9	111.5	109.9	108.6	109.6	110.8	110.9	110.5	109.3	108.8
1926	110.2	110.8	109.6	110.1	110.2	110.2	110.0	110.2	110.0	110.2	109.3	109.3
1927	111.3	110.5	110.3	110.6	110.6	110.1	110.3	110.6	110.7	111.9	110.6	111.2
1928	112.4	112.3	112.4	113.7	112.4	112.4	112.1	112.1	111.7	112.3	112.1	112.1
1929	113.4	111.7	111.1	111.9	110.4	109.8	109.3	109.0	108.9	109.3	108.5	108.5
1930	109.6	110.1	112.7	112.7	111.4	110.0	112.3	111.9	112.0	113.1	112.8	112.5
1931	112.8	109.7	111.6	111.3	110.8	111.1	111.2	107.2	103.5	104.2	104.8	102.2
1932	104.7	106.5	111.6	110.6	111.4	111.0	115.6	116.1	118.4	120.3	115.9	116.1
1933	116.9	118.4	118.4	120.2	118.1	118.7	117.9	120.1	121.2	122.3	122.3	122.0
1934	123.6	124.3	126.2	126.9	125.8	125.3	127.1	127.4	128.3	128.9	133.2	132.7
1935	134.6	131.6	130.3	131.3	131.3	130.3	131.5	129.8	124.3	125.5	128.9	129.5
1936	130.1	131.0	130.2	131.5	131.1	130.6	131.0	131.6	132.1	132.9	132.0	130.9
1937	129.7	125.5	124.8	125.3	125.0	123.9	123.3	123.2	122.8	123.6	124.1	123.9
1938	124.7	125.1	121.0	124.2	122.1	121.9	123.4	122.4	118.4	118.2	118.0	116.3
1939	115.9	115.8	113.6	110.8	113.5	113.5	112.5	110.9	106.9	109.5	112.3	112.4

TABLE 8.7 : INDEX OF THE VALUE OF VARIABLE - INTEREST SECURITIES
(DECEMBER 1921 = 100)

	JAN	FEB	MAR	APR	MAY	JUN	JUL	AUG	SEP	OCT	NOV	DEC
1922	101.3	102.8	105.9	114.1	114.9	114.4	116.7	118.2	119.7	121.0	119.5	117.6
1923	118.0	120.2	121.8	124.4	123.2	122.7	117.5	115.8	117.4	117.0	117.1	115.9
1924	116.9	120.5	119.3	119.5	119.7	119.9	120.4	121.6	120.7	121.9	126.2	126.9
1925	129.0	129.2	127.2	126.9	125.6	125.5	124.2	127.1	126.6	129.5	132.2	132.5
1926	132.6	131.6	129.2	128.7	131.0	133.6	132.8	135.4	136.5	134.5	135.9	135.7
1927	138.5	139.9	139.0	140.4	141.6	141.5	142.0	142.9	144.2	146.0	145.9	146.9
1928	147.9	147.7	151.7	154.7	157.8	152.7	151.7	154.2	156.7	158.7	159.4	158.8
1929	163.4	162.0	161.1	159.5	157.4	157.9	162.0	164.4	165.4	160.8	147.0	147.1
1930	146.7	146.3	145.3	147.9	143.7	135.5	137.2	131.0	134.6	127.0	125.2	118.5
1931	119.2	118.8	119.0	113.3	102.2	103.6	105.4	98.2	89.5	100.6	99.4	90.7
1932	92.8	91.7	92.7	84.5	92.0	78.9	84.5	92.5	96.8	96.3	96.8	95.8
1933	96.4	96.1	96.2	96.3	100.4	105.0	111.7	112.4	113.5	110.4	107.7	108.4
1934	113.8	115.8	116.2	117.3	115.9	114.5	112.9	111.6	111.3	112.5	113.9	113.5
1935	115.7	113.7	110.0	111.5	114.4	115.6	115.6	117.5	112.7	112.6	118.3	120.1
1936	123.9	126.7	125.2	127.1	124.8	125.1	126.1	129.5	130.7	135.9	137.4	137.7
1937	138.7	138.2	136.7	134.4	132.2	129.1	128.9	128.8	123.4	117.4	114.3	115.5
1938	115.1	111.5	105.0	108.8	106.1	104.5	109.3	108.0	104.4	106.0	107.0	104.4
1939	103.8	103.2	102.6	100.0	102.5	101.9	100.9	100.2	95.8	99.7	101.1	100.8

TABLE 8.8 : INDEX OF THE VALUE OF SECURITIES
(DECEMBER 1921 = 100)

	JAN	FEB	MAR	APR	MAY	JUN	JUL	AUG	SEP	OCT	NOV	DEC
1922	102.1	105.8	107.3	113.3	113.4	112.8	114.4	114.7	114.0	115.1	114.1	113.2
1923	114.2	115.3	116.4	119.0	118.0	118.0	114.1	114.4	115.5	115.5	113.6	112.8
1924	112.2	114.3	114.2	115.6	115.3	115.3	115.2	115.8	115.6	116.2	117.4	117.5
1925	117.5	117.9	116.9	116.5	115.1	114.1	114.4	116.2	116.0	116.7	116.8	116.5
1926	117.5	117.6	116.0	116.2	117.0	117.9	117.5	118.4	118.7	118.2	118.0	118.0
1927	120.2	120.2	119.7	120.4	120.7	120.4	120.7	121.2	121.9	123.1	122.2	122.8
1928	124.0	123.9	125.3	127.1	127.2	125.4	124.9	125.7	126.3	127.3	127.4	127.3
1929	129.6	128.1	127.3	127.3	125.6	125.4	126.5	127.0	127.3	126.1	120.9	121.0
1930	121.7	121.8	123.3	124.2	121.9	119.0	120.3	118.1	119.3	117.6	116.8	114.4
1931	114.9	112.6	114.1	111.9	108.0	108.6	109.3	104.3	99.0	103.1	103.1	98.5
1932	100.9	101.7	105.5	102.1	101.8	100.6	105.5	108.4	111.4	112.5	109.6	109.4
1933	110.2	111.1	111.2	112.4	112.5	114.3	115.9	117.6	118.7	118.4	117.6	117.6
1934	120.4	121.5	122.9	123.8	122.6	121.8	122.5	122.3	122.8	123.6	126.9	126.5
1935	128.5	125.8	123.7	124.9	125.8	125.5	126.4	125.8	120.6	121.3	125.5	126.4
1936	128.1	129.6	128.6	130.1	129.1	128.8	129.4	131.0	131.7	133.9	133.8	133.1
1937	132.6	129.7	128.4	128.2	127.3	125.6	125.1	125.0	123.0	121.6	121.0	121.2
1938	121.6	120.7	115.9	119.2	117.0	116.3	118.9	117.7	113.8	114.2	114.4	112.4
1939	112.0	111.7	110.0	107.1	110.0	109.8	108.8	107.4	103.3	106.3	108.7	108.7

TABLE 8.9 : INDEX OF PROFITS (ECONOMIST)
(JULY 1935 - JUNE 1936 AVERAGE = 100)

	MAR	JUN	SEP	DEC
1929			113.0	113.1
1930	113.8	116.5	115.5	111.7
1931	107.4	101.3	93.6	87.2
1932	81.7	73.3	69.9	69.1
1933	66.3	67.6	66.8	68.5
1934	70.1	74.6	76.7	79.7
1935	83.8	88.9	90.2	92.4
1936	96.6	100.0	102.0	104.5
1937	108.6	118.3	120.9	125.2
1938	128.7	131.7	131.6	130.3
1939	127.1	122.9	121.8	119.6

Index

Page numbers in italic indicate references to tables